Vauxhall Viva

Covers all models HA/HB/HC with ohv engines, 1963-77

(Does not cover 1600, 1800 or 2300 ohc models)

Owner's Handbook/Servicing Guide

by I M Coomber

2185/385

Haynes

Acknowledgements

Thanks are due to Vauxhall Motors Ltd for the supply of technical information and illustrations, and to Wincanton Garages Ltd of Yeovil who supplied the Viva used for many of the photographs.

Valued advice was given by Castrol Ltd on lubrication, and by the Champion Sparking Plug Company on spark plug conditions.

Thanks are also due to all the people at Sparkford who helped in the production of this Handbook, including Brian Horsfall who carried out the various service and maintenance operations in our workshops, and photographer Leon Martindale (a member of the Master Photographers' Association). The layout of the pages was planned by Lee Saunders.

A book in the Haynes Owners Handbook/Servicing Guide Series

Edited by Robin Wager

Published and printed by the Haynes Publishing Group, Sparkford, Yeovil, Somerset BA22 7JJ

ISBN 0 85696 385 2

Contents

1974 HC Viva de Luxe

What's in it for You?

Whether you've bought this book yourself or had it given to you, the idea was probably the same in either case – to help you get the best out of your Viva and perhaps to make motoring a bit less of a drain on your hard-earned cash at the same time.

Garage labour charges can easily be several times your own hourly rate of pay, and usually form the main part of any servicing bill; we'll help you avoid them by carrying out the routine services yourself. Even if you *don't* want to do the regular servicing, and prefer to leave it to your Vauxhall dealer, there are some things you should check regularly just to make sure that your car's not a danger to you or to anyone else on the road; we tell you what they are.

If you're about to start doing your own servicing (whether to cut costs or to be sure that it's done properly) we think you'll find the procedures described give an easy-to-follow introduction to what can be a very satisfying way of spending a few hours of your spare time.

We've included some tips that should save you some money when buying replacement parts and even while you're driving; there's a chapter on cleaning and renovating your car, and another on fitting accessories.

Apart from the things every Viva owner needs to know to deal with mishaps like a puncture or a broken headlamp, we've put together some Troubleshooter Charts to cover the more likely of the problems that can crop up with even the most carefully maintained car sooner or later, and there's a comprehensive alphabetical index to help you find your way around the book.

If the bug gets you, and you're keen to tackle some of the more advanced repair jobs on your car, then you'll need one of the Haynes Owners Workshop manuals covering the Viva range which give a step-by-step guide to all the repair and overhaul tasks on these cars, with plenty of illustrations to make things even clearer.

Viva 1300 GLS Saloon

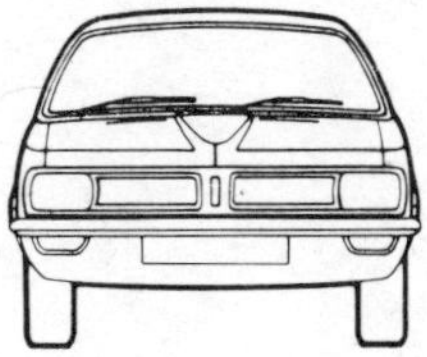

The Viva Family

The Viva was introduced as the HA model in 1963 and was Vauxhall's first venture into the compact engine vehicle range for many years. Individual in character, it aroused a lot of interest and was an immediate success. Apart from its stylish lines it was obviously designed to be practical rather than trendy; unlike many other 'compacts' being produced at that time, the Viva was quite conventional in layout, having a four cylinder water-cooled in-line engine with overhead valves. The transmission had four forward and one reverse gear, with synchromesh on all forward gears.

The power was transmitted to the rear axle via a normal propeller shaft with universal joints. Drum brakes were fitted all round, and the steering was by rack and pinion. The front suspension was independent with short and long arms, a transverse spring and telescopic shock absorbers. The rear suspension had semi-elliptic springs with telescopic shock absorbers.

The bodywork was quite spacious for it's size and the lines were simple but effective.Originally two basic models were produced, the Standard saloon and the De Luxe saloon. Mechanically identical, the

The HB Viva de Luxe

1974 HC Viva SL Estate

The HA series Viva SL

De Luxe version incorporated extra refinements such as a heater (!) and screenwash. A Super luxury saloon (SL) version was introduced in June 1965 and in October of that year, higher performance engine versions became available in the '90' De Luxe and '90' Super De Luxe models, which had uprated engines and servo-assisted brakes. Over 300,000 of the HA Viva saloons left the production lines during the three years in which the model was manufactured.

A Bedford van version of the HA was also produced in 1964, and has continued in production since, with the later engines fitted to the original body design. The 6 cwt and 8 cwt models were designated HAE and HAV respectively, while an Estate version of this vehicle (no longer produced) was called the 'Bedford Beagle'. Recently the vans have undergone cosmetic treatment, mainly to the interior trim and fittings, and the specified payloads have been uprated. The available models now are the HA 110 (payload 371 kg/7.2 cwt) and the HA 130 (546 kg/10.8 cwt). Both have the same 1256 cc engine, with a special economy version optional on the HA 110.

Servicing procedures on the HA series vans are similar to those for the saloons.

Viva HB (August 1966 to October 1970)

In August 1966 the HB Viva was introduced, with a redesigned bodyshell having more flowing lines than the HA series and rectangular headlights. Initially, five models were available, the Standard saloon, the De Luxe saloon, the SL and, for the sporty minded types with a slightly fatter bank balance, a '90' version of the De Luxe and SL models.

The engine capacity was increased from 1057 cc (HA series) to 1159 cc and the new body was $6\frac{1}{2}$ inches longer than the HA. The independent front suspension was modified and the rear suspension was now independent too, with coil springs and telescopic shock absorbers.

In 1967, a Borg Warner automatic transmission became available as an option, and Estate versions of the De Luxe, SL and '90' variants were introduced. The estate specifications are basically the same as the saloons except that they have higher-rate springs and a heavy duty rear axle.

In 1968 a four-door body was made available on all models with the exception of the Standard saloon and Estate. An energy-absorbing steering column was now fitted to all models, and the facia switches and controls were relocated.

Viva HC (Oct 1970 onwards)

A restyled body was introduced for both the saloon and estate versions, allowing additional passenger space. The principal identification features of the new body are the 'square' headlights and wrap-around tail light units, and a pronounced ridge on the bonnet centre line. The engine was uprated for the SL90 versions and the heating and ventilation system modified. A GM type 3-speed automatic transmission was offered in place of the Borg Warner type.

In September 1971 the 1256 cc engine was introduced, replacing the standard and '90' versions previously installed. The automatic and manual transmissions together with the rear axle were strengthened to cope with the additional engine power.

In 1972, power-assisted dual-circuit disc and drum brakes were fitted to all models.

For the 1973 range the transmission and axle were further strengthened. The compression ratio was increased from 8.5 to 9.2 and the carburettor, inlet and exhaust manifolds modified.

More recently the range has been newly subdivided and the available models are now 1300E, 1300L and 1300 GLS, the level of trim and standard fittings becoming progressively better in that order. The L and GLS versions are also available as Estates, and all models except the E have radial ply tyres as standard.

Road Test Data Taken From Autocar

The figures published here are extracts from *Autocar* magazine road tests.

Fuel consumption: The mpg figure is the overall consumption figure for their test period, including performance testing. Many owners will achieve significantly better consumption figures. The formula on the right provides a guide ('**mpg**' refers to the quoted overall test figure).

Driving style	*Driving conditions* severe	average	easy
Hard	−10%	**mpg**	+10%
Average	**mpg**	+10%	+20%
Gentle	+10%	+20%	+30%

	HA Viva de luxe (1057cc)	**HB Viva de luxe (1159cc)**	**HC Viva de luxe (1159cc)**	**HC Viva SL (1256cc)**
Maximum speed (mph)	76	78	79	84
Overall fuel consumption (mpg)	31.4	28.1	29.3	24.2
Fuel consumption at constant:				
30 mph (mpg)	49.0	55.6	52.0	55.5
50 mph	40.0	43.0	43.1	43.5
70 mph	28.0	29.0	27.6	27.0
Range on full fuel tank (miles)	219	224	234	248
Acceleration (seconds):				
0–30 mph	5.2	5.0	5.6	5.0
0–40 mph	8.6	7.9	9.1	7.6
0–50 mph	13.7	13.1	14.3	12.0
0–60 mph	22.1	19.7	21.3	17.6
0–70 mph	36.2	33.7	37.0	29.7
Standing start $\frac{1}{4}$ mile	21.5	21.0	21.8	20.3
40–60 mph in top gear	17.6	17.0	17.5	14.7

In the Driving Seat

Apart from the modifications mentioned previously, various changes have been made in the Viva's interior and controls layout over the years. The experienced motorist will probably be familiar with most of the controls and instruments as they're pretty straightforward, but a brief rundown may be useful to anyone who has borrowed or recently acquired a Viva and isn't familiar with some of its finer points.

Ignition warning light

The ignition warning light indicates one of two things. First it reminds the driver that the ignition circuit's switched on (though the engine may not be running). Secondly it indicates that the charging circuit's inoperative and therefore in need of attention.

The ignition warning light should glow only when the ignition's switched on with the engine stopped, or when the engine's idling very slowly. As soon as the engine speed is increased to anything above idling speed the warning light should go out. If the light stays on with increased engine speed, then the charging circuit must be inspected as soon as possible, otherwise the battery will eventually lose its charge.

It's not advisable to leave the ignition switch in the 'on' position with the engine stopped, as apart from draining power from the battery, the ignition system wiring may overheat.

Oil pressure warning light or oil pressure gauge

When the ignition is first switched on the oil pressure warning light should glow, but as soon as the engine starts the light should go out and stay out. If it stays on, comes on when driving or possibly flickers at engine idling speed, this indicates that the engine oil pressure is dangerously low owing to lack of oil in the sump or mechanical wear or damage. Whatever the cause, if the light comes on while you're driving, switch off the engine and pull off the road as soon as is safely possible. If the warning light came on to the accompaniment of loud knocking noises from the engine department, don't attempt to

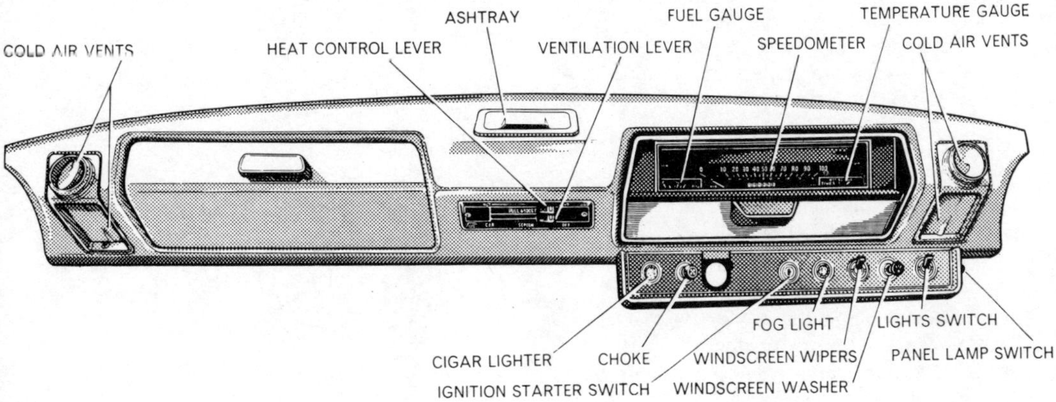

The instrument panel and switches – HB model

drive the car any further! Whatever the circumstances, investigate the cause of the oil light coming on and, if in doubt, don't run the engine again until expert assistance has been obtained.

If an oil pressure gauge is fitted, this will give a clear indication of whether there's a partial or full loss in oil pressure. When the engine's running at 3000 revolutions per minute the oil pressure gauge should indicate a reading of 35 to 45 psi.

Temperature gauge (when fitted)

The temperature gauge won't operate unless the ignition's switched on. The gauge indicates the temperature of the coolant in the cooling system. Normally the needle should hover around the centre of the scale once the engine's warmed up. Should the needle stay in the 'cool' position after a few miles' running, then this indicates that the thermostat in the cooling system is faulty and should be checked as soon as possible. If the needle moves to the right of the gauge then the coolant is approaching or has reached boiling point, and you should stop to investigate the cause. **Extra care must be taken when checking the coolant level if the engine's hot** – see *Filling Station Facts* for the right way to do it.

Switches

Most switches are self-explanatory in operation, but it's worth mentioning one or two peculiarities. On HA models, the two rocker switches fitted to operate the side and headlights are interconnected so that when the headlight switch is pressed to the 'ON' position, the sidelight switch is automatically operated too. However, the sidelight switch can be used separately when required.

All models are fitted with the all-in-one headlight dipper/flasher, direction indicator and horn switch mounted on the steering column; the single stalk will operate one or all three simultaneously as required. A self-cancelling mechanism's incorporated in the indicator unit.

The instrument panel light switch is at the lower edge of the panel. Both this and the side-light switch must be in the 'On' position before the instruments will light up.

Steering column lock

Certain HB models and all HC models are fitted with a combined steering column lock and ignition/starter switch. Three types have been used. With the first, the steering's locked by turning the ignition key to the 'Lock' position, and withdrawing the key. The steering wheel's then turned until it clicks into the locked position. To unlock the steering, insert the key and turn it to the 'Off' position. If the

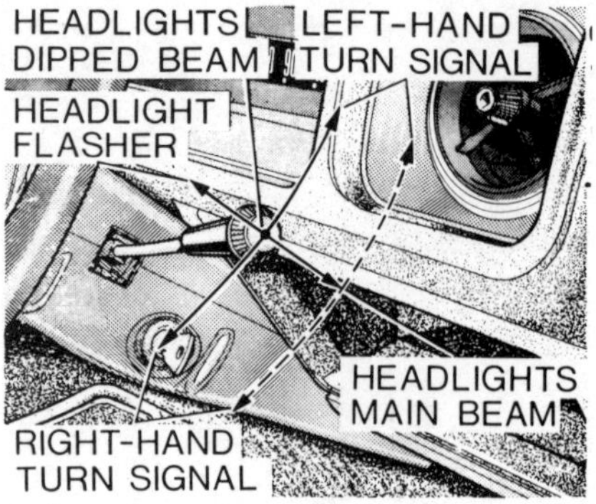

The combination switch positions – (HC model)

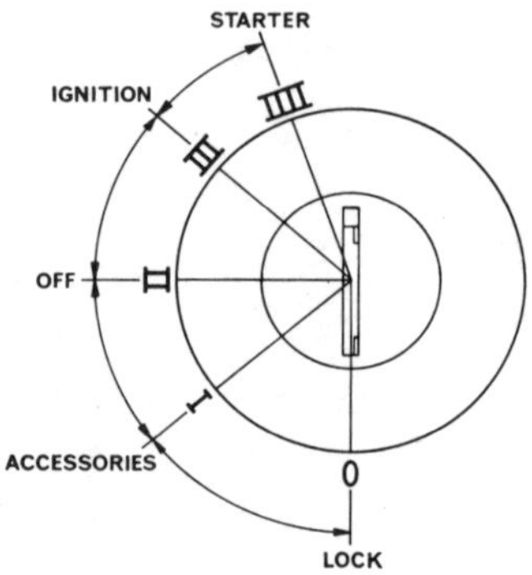

The ignition switch positions – HB models

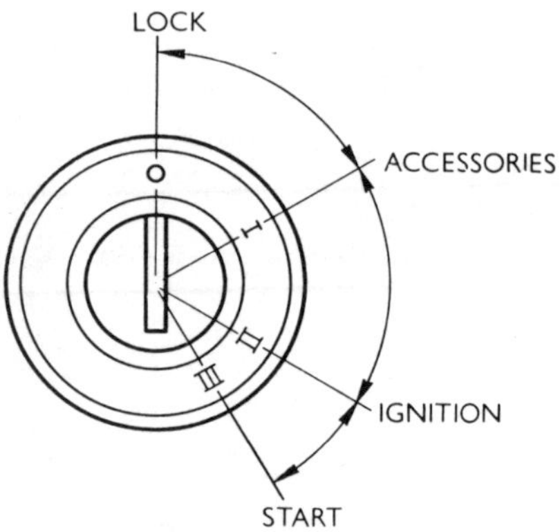

The ignition switch positions – HC models

Interior of 1969 HB Viva de Luxe

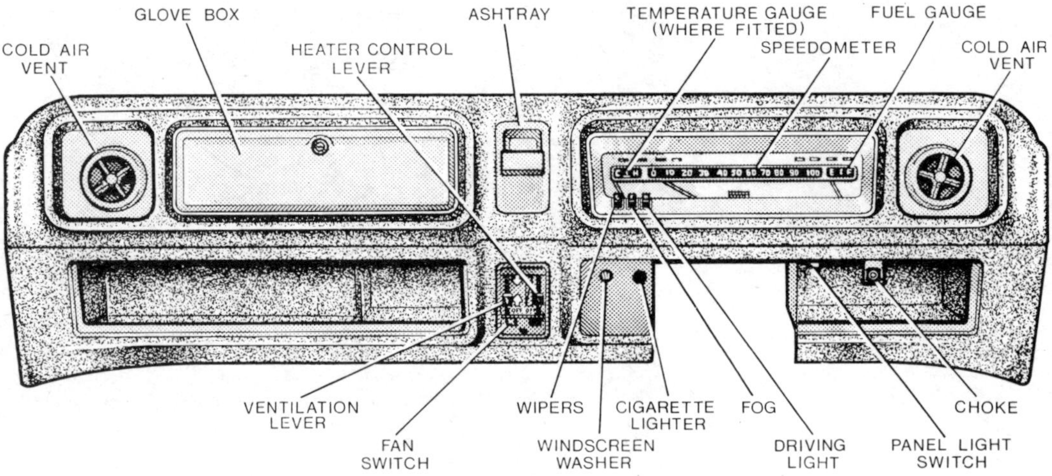

The instrument panel and switches - HC models

Interior of 1974 HC Viva SL

key's difficult to turn, 'rock' the steering wheel back and forth slightly whilst turning the key clockwise.

On the second type the key's turned from the 'Ignition/Accessories' position until a slight resistance is felt, then pressed in and turned further so that it aligns with the 'O'(lock) position. Take out the key to lock the steering. Unlocking's the reverse procedure. The key can only be inserted and removed in the 'O' (lock) position, and it may be necessary to rock the steering wheel to turn the key.

Note: Never tow the vehicle with the key set in the 'O' (lock) position and never move the key to the 'O' position when in motion!

The latest type ignition lock incorporates a safety button underneath the steering column shroud which must be pressed in before the key can be taken out. This really calls for the use of two hands and effectively prevents the steering being locked inadvertently while the car's moving.

Keys

Loss of the ignition (or, for that matter, the door/boot key) can prove rather inconvenient and sometimes embarrassing! There are no lock serial numbers on the lock barrels, for security reasons, so unless you know the key number(s) you're in trouble! Even knowing the numbers does not necessarily mean that you'll be able to get an over-the-counter replacement, so it's a good idea to always carry a spare ignition and door key with you (not in the car!) or at least record the numbers for emergency use.

Choke controls

Manual choke (HA, HB and manual transmission HC models):

The manually operated choke should only be used for starting the engine when cold. Once the engine's started the choke should be used just as long as is necessary for the engine to reach a reasonable operating temperature, and then should be pushed fully in again. Continued use of the choke when the engine's operating normally will only waste fuel and cause unnecessary engine wear.

Many drivers have a habit of pumping the accelerator continuously when starting the engine, and this is to be avoided. Apart from exercising the right foot, it only induces the carburettor to flood the engine with excessive fuel which makes starting more difficult. If, however, the energetic action appears to be the only way to start the car, it indicates that the carburettor's badly adjusted and should be serviced at the earliest opportunity.

To clear a 'flooded' engine, push the choke knob fully in, press the accelerator *slowly* down to its fullest extent and hold it there whilst operating the starter. This should help to clear the excess petrol and enable the engine to start.

Automatic choke:

An automatic choke's fitted to all HC models with the GM automatic transmission and eliminates the need for a control knob The automatic choke fully controls the fuel/air mixture to the engine as required, according to conditions. When the engine's started from cold, the accelerator pedal must be pressed down fully and then released, which sets the automatic choke to enable the engine to start and run at a fast idle speed. The idle speed will progressively drop as the engine's warmed up. If after the initial attempt the engine fails to start, don't continue to pump the accelerator pedal as this will only cause the engine to flood and make matters worse. Allow the starter motor to disengage and the engine to stop turning, and then operate the starter again.

Automatic transmission

An automatic transmission system's available as an option to the manual gearbox fitted as standard. Two types of automatic transmission have been used, the Borg-Warner automatic on the earlier types and the GM automatic currently in use. The principles of operation of both types are the same, with a fluid torque converter acting as a clutch to transmit the engine power to the automatic gearbox.

The operation of the automatic gearbox is different from that of the manual transmission and for anybody who's not familiar with this type of gearbox, the functions of the various selector positions are as follows:

'P' Park: In this position, whether the engine's stopped or running, no gears are engaged and transmission's mechanically locked. The car can't be moved although the engine can be started. In order to select the 'P' position, the button on the selector lever must be fully pressed in. Don't select 'P' if the car's moving or damage will result.

'N' Neutral: The same as for 'P' except that the transmission's not locked. The car will therefore roll with the engine either running or stopped.

'R' Reverse: In this position reverse gear is engaged. With the brakes applied, the car won't move, but when they're released and the engine speeded up a little the car will move backwards. In order to engage 'R' the button on the selector lever must be partially pressed in. If the engine's not running, it can't be started unless 'P' or 'N' is first selected.

'D' Drive: This is the selector position for normal driving. In this position, first gear is initially engaged (though at idling speed with the brakes released the car may roll either forward or backward). When the engine's speeded up a little the car will move forward.

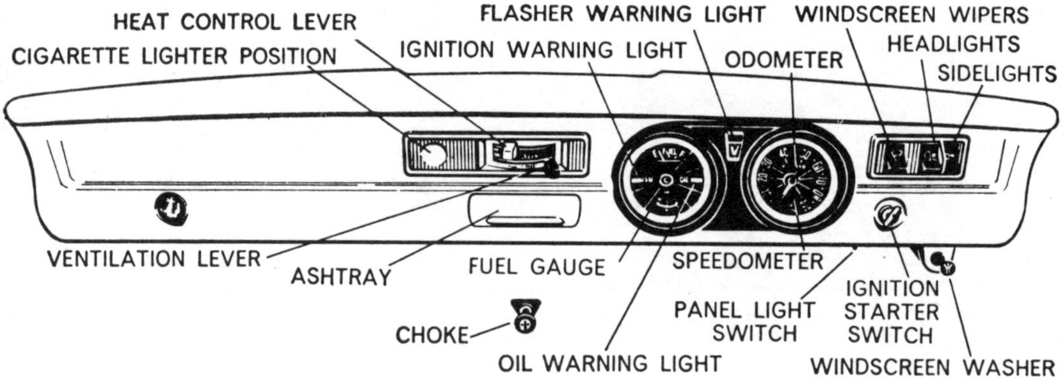

The instrument panel and switches - HA model

Interior of the 1977 Viva 1300 GLS

As the speed and load conditions change, the gears will automatically change up and down as required. The engine doesn't act as a brake on over-run in any of the three speeds in the 'D' position.

'I' Intermediate: To select this position the lever button must be partially pressed in. When selected, the transmission will operate as in 'D' except that it won't move up out of 2nd gear. It shouldn't be used in excess of 60 mph.

It's possible to change to 'I' when the car's moving; this will immediately put it into 2nd gear unless until speed or throttle position cause it to change down to 1st. The Intermediate range is normally used in traffic or on uphill stretches where the 'D' position would give a lot of changing up and down between 2nd and top gears. In the 'I' position there's engine braking on the over-run in 2nd gear, but not in 1st.

'L' Low: To select this position the lever button must be fully pressed in. It shouldn't be selected above 35 mph, and would normally be used to provide engine braking on steep downhill stretches or to avoid unnecessary changing between 1st and 2nd gears in dense traffic or on continuous slow climbs. As suggested, there is engine braking on the over-run in 'L'.

'Kickdown' facility: It's possible to obtain a more-or-less instant changedown, to give extra acceleration for overtaking, for example, by pressing the accelerator pedal fully down. This changedown won't happen, however, if the car's already travelling at more than the maximum speed for the lower gear.

There are one or two other points in connection with automatic transmission that should be borne in mind by newcomers and more experienced owners alike, to avoid unwanted problems. For example:

(a) Cars fitted with automatic transmission also have an automatic choke on the carburettor so that engine speed is suitably increased until it's warmed up. There will be a tendency to a fastertickover for a while after starting from cold, which in turn will cause the car to 'creep' when any of the driving ranges is selected, unless the brakes are firmly applied. This may even be so to a lesser extent with a fully warm engine; it's quite normal, and can even be useful when manoeuvring in tight spaces! Because of the effect of engine speed on the transmission, tuning and carburettor adjustment are much more important with an automatic car.

(b) The 'L' or 'I' range must be selected to get continuous engine braking on over-run, and when shifting into either of these while on the move a deceleration will occur. Remember that on slippery surfaces there's a possibility of a skid occurring due to the sudden braking effect on the back wheels.

(c) It's not possible to start the engine of an automatic model by towing or pushing. If the car has to be towed owing to a breakdown, the speed should be kept below 30 mph and the selector placed in 'N'. Not more than 30 miles should be covered in this way, to avoid overheating. If there's a suspected fault in the transmission, the car shouldn't be towed at all unless the propeller shaft's disconnected or the back wheels raised clear of the ground to prevent the transmission turning.

Filling Station Facts

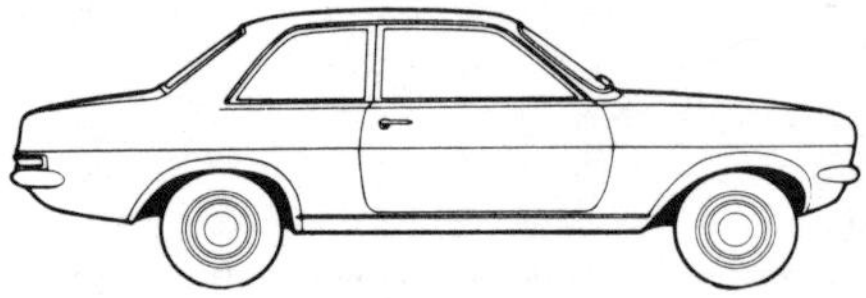

Forgetting about the actual servicing and mechanical maintenance of your car for the time being, there are some things which are so simple they're likely to get overlooked; but they're not only an important part of the maintenance of your car – they're vital for its safety and reliability too. Three of these items – tyres, oil and water – you can check if necessary whenever you visit a petrol station.

We've set out here the absolute minimum of information you need right from the very first day you drive a Viva.

Topping up oil

Whenever you top up the oil level, always try to use the same grade and brand; and do avoid using cheap oil – the initial saving will probably be lost in increased engine wear over a prolonged period – or perhaps a short one!

When checking the oil level, ensure that the car's standing on level ground. Take out the dipstick, wipe it clean, then replace it fully. Pull it out again and note the oil level. Under no circumstances should the level be allowed to drop below the ADD OIL mark. If the oil level is at this mark, 2 pints will be needed to bring it up to FULL. Avoid over-filling and wipe up any oil spilt.

Checking tyre pressure

Checking coolant level

If the engine's at its normal running temperature or higher, **take extra care** when removing the radiator filler cap. Place a rag over the cap, turn slowly anti-clockwise to the first position, and allow the pressure in the system to escape, then again turn anticlockwise and remove carefully.

If a considerable amount of water's required to top up or you're continuously adding water during the winter months, the antifreeze mixture will be diluted and made less effective. So if antifreeze is in use, topping up should be done with water/antifreeze mixture in the correct proportions.

The coolant level should be brought up to 1inch (25 mm) below the bottom of the filler neck. Make sure that the radiator cap's properly fitted afterwards.

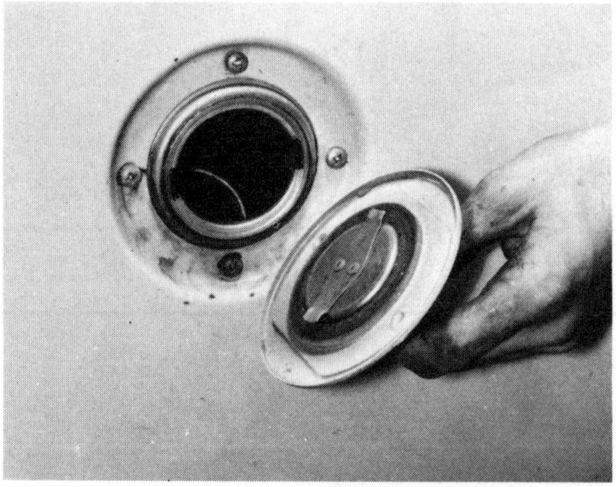

Fuel filler cap location (nearside rear wing)

Tyre pressures

When checking tyre pressures don't forget to check the pressure in the spare – in the event of a

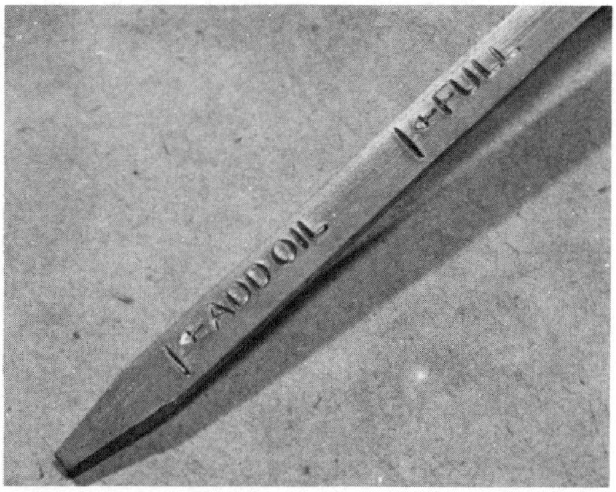

Dipstick check

puncture you could be in for a 'let down'! If you're affluent enough to have your own tyre pressure gauge, always use this to check the pressures – garage gauges aren't always terribly accurate and it's essential that the pressures are right to ensure the correct handling of the car when steering and braking.

Remember that tyre pressures can only be checked accurately when the tyres are cold. Any tyre that's travelled more than a mile or so will show a pressure increase of several pounds per square inch (psi) – maybe more than 5 psi after a longer run. So a certain amount of 'guesstimation' comes into checking tyres if they're warm.

Since the pressures won't increase for any reason other than heat, the least you can do is to ensure that the pressures in the two front tyres are equal, bearing in mind that they may be a bit above those shown in the table. (The same applies to the two back tyres, but remember that their pressure should be different from the front).

If one tyre of a pair has a low pressure when hot, bring it up to the pressure of the other at the same end of the car; if they're both below the recommended cold pressure although warm, the safest thing to do is to bring them up to about 3 psi above it, to allow for cooling.

Self-service garages

Many garages now operate on a self-service basis so that the customer's subjected to the intricacies of refuelling his or her own vehicle. Regulars to this type of establishment need no introduction to its methods of operation and can usually be seen going through the routine at high speed like well-oiled robots. To the newcomer, the operation of the various kinds of pump can at first be confusing, but don't panic! Carefully read each instruction on the pump in turn before attempting to work it. When refuelling, insert the nozzle fully into the car's filler tube and try to regulate the fuel flow at an even rate so that it's not too fast. Most pumps now have an automatic flow-back valve mechanism fitted in them, which prevents any surplus petrol making a speedy exit from the filler neck all over the unsuspecting operator. On completion, don't forget to refit your petrol filler cap!

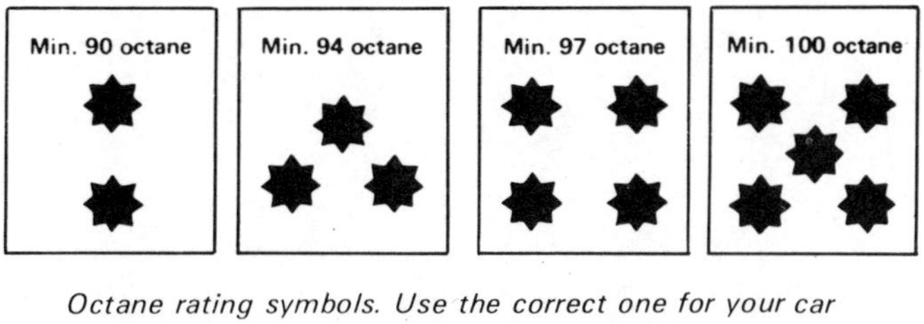

Octane rating symbols. Use the correct one for your car

QUICK-CHECK CHART

	VIVA HA		VIVA HB		VIVA HC	
TYRE PRESSURES						
Recommended pressures in psi (kg/cm^2) when cold F = Front R = Rear	F	R	F	R	F	R
Saloon except SL models (normal conditions)	18 (1.26)	22 (1.55)	22 (1.55)	22 (1.55)	24 (1.69)	24 (1.69)
Saloon incl. SL (prolonged high speeds or max. load)	22 (1.55)	26 (1.83)	22 (1.55)	22 (1.55)	24 (1.69)	30 (2.11)
Estate (normal)	–	–	24 (1.69)	26 (1.83)	22 (1.55)	22 (1.55)
Estate (max. load/heavy duty)	–	–	24 (1.69)	28 (1.97)	24 (1.69)	30 (2.11)
Van HAE (normal)	20 (1.41)	36 (2.52)				
Van HAE (prolonged high speeds or max. load)	20 (1.41)	40 (2.82)				
Van HAV (normal)	20 (1.41)	40 (2.82)				
Van HAV (prolonged high speeds or max. load)	20 (1.41)	45 (3.16)				
SL models (normal conditions) and all vehicles with optional 165/70 HR radial tyres (all conditions)			22	22	22	22
FUEL OCTANE RATING (min)						
9.2 and 8.5 compression ratio	97 (4 star)		97 (4 star)		97 (4 star)	
7.3 compression ratio	90 (2 star)		90 (2 star)		90 (2 star)	
FUEL TANK CAPACITY	7 gal (31.8 litres)		8 gal (36.4 litres)		8 gal (36.4 litres)	
ENGINE OIL TYPE	20W/50 Multigrade		20W/50 Multigrade		20W/50 Multigrade	
QUANTITY OF OIL REQUIRED TO BRING LEVEL FROM 'ADD OIL' TO 'FULL' ON DIPSTICK	2 pints (1.1 litres)		2 pints (1.1 litres)		2 pints (1.1 litres)	

In an Emergency

Servicing tasks and intervals have fortunately become fewer over the years, and consequently what was at one time a weekly 'rebuild' has become for many an optimistic motorist the annual chore, and this only because the MoT test is coming up! Small wonder then that the occasional spot of bother or breakdown still occurs, when the specified service checks and jobs are ignored, and this fact is even boasted about by many people.

This does not of course apply to everybody. A lot of owners religiously check, service and clean their car at regular intervals, and some almost wrap it up in the proverbial cotton wool each night.

However, even the most carefully looked-after car will let you down some day. Punctures are still a common event, and although changing a wheel isn't the major operation it used to be, it's still not a pastime to be recommended, especially as it always seems to need doing on a cold wet night; and you won't feel any better with your spouse or mother-in-law looking on in scorn as you discover that the spare's flat and you've no idea how the jack works. If you're not familiar with the jack supplied with your Viva, read on – because one day you're going to need to use it!

Jacking up and changing a wheel

Whenever the car's to be jacked up (either to change a wheel or for any other purpose) the car must be parked on firm, flat ground. The jack supplied with the vehicle is intended only for raising the car in the event of a puncture to change the wheel. It shouldn't be used to lift the car to perform any major tasks underneath unless it is further supported with chassis stands or blocks to make it secure.

Before jacking up, make sure the handbrake's firmly applied, engage first gear, and place block of some description each side of the wheel diagonally opposed to the one to be changed.

The wheelnut spanner has a specially shaped blade on its end and this is used as a lever to remove the hub plate from the wheel. Insert the blade

Levering off wheel trim plate

Slackening the wheel nuts

Spare wheel location

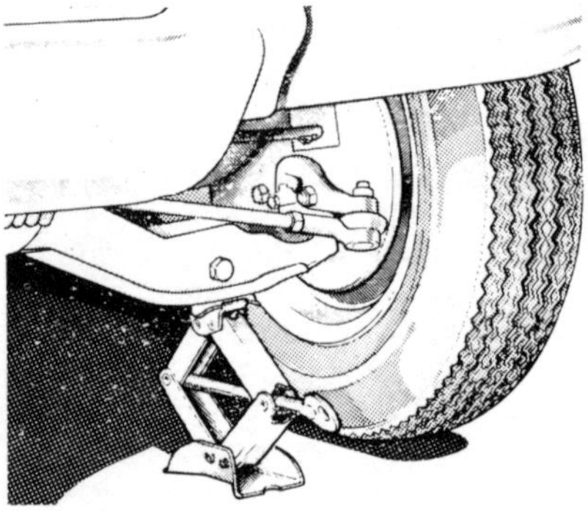

Jack position – front

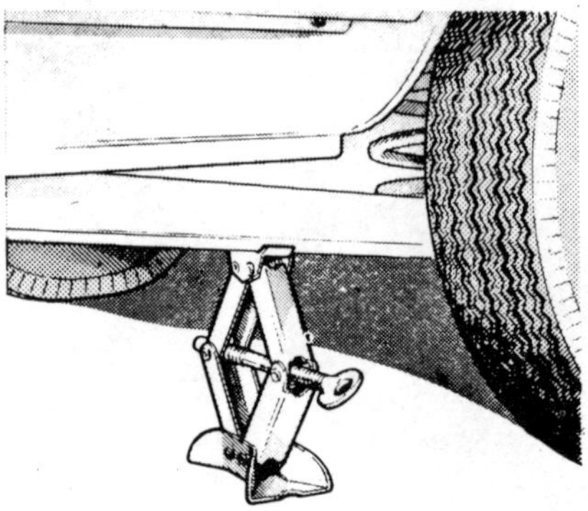

Jack position – rear

between the wheel and hub plate, position the socket end of the spanner against the tyre, and tap the socket end to spring the hub plate free. To avoid scratching the hub plate place a piece of rag on the ground for it to land on.

The wheelnuts are now accessible, and each nut should be loosened about half a turn. If the nuts are reluctant to move under hand pressure, try using your foot on the spanner, but take care that it doesn't slip off the nut in the process.

Place the jack securely in position. When raising a front wheel the jack must be placed under the lower front suspension arm; the rear wheels are raised with the jack under the rear suspension arm adjacent to the rear axle.

Having raised the jack, check that it's secure and the wheel chocks are still in position, then take off the wheel nuts and wheel.

Fit the spare wheel, and finger tighten the nuts (ensuring that their domed ends face the wheel) then lower and remove the jack. The wheelnuts must now be fully tightened. Don't bend the spanner doing this – just make sure they're firmly tight but remember they'll have to come off again sometime! (It's not absolutely necessary, but advisable, to recheck the nuts for tightness, later after some miles have covered). Finally, refit the hub plate and remove chocks.

Maintenance of Lights

Failure of any of the car's external lights can not only lay you open to prosecution if you're driving, but also constitutes a safety hazard. It's for this reason that we recommend carrying a spare set of the main bulbs, and their replacement has been included in this Chapter as we think a lamp failure should be regarded as an emergency. For your own safety as well as everyone else's, don't let your Viva join the large number of vehicles that can be seen driving around any night after dark with one or more of the obligatory lights not working. Here's how to prevent it.

Headlamp/Sidelamp bulb replacement

HA Series

Remove the retaining screw from the headlamp surround trim. Now unscrew the three crosshead screws holding the lamp unit in position – (not the beam alignment adjusting screws). Withdraw the lamp unit and pull off the connection block. Release the bulb retaining clips and take out the bulb. When fitting the new bulb ensure that the bulb flange is properly engaged in the body slot.

With the exception of the very early models, the front sidelight bulbs are housed in the reflector. To remove the sidelight on this type, pull the claw-type

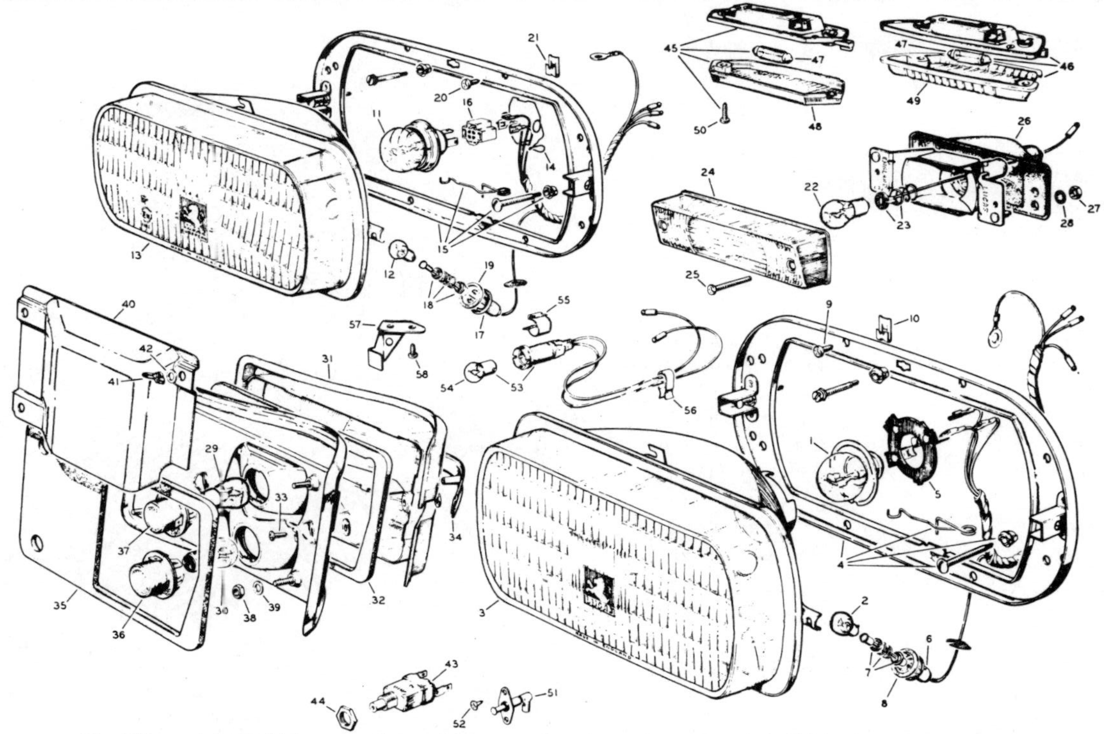

The HB model headlights, rear lights, indicators, interior and number plate lights component parts

1 Headlamp bulb (UK)
2 Sidelamp bulb
3 Headlamp lens
4 Mounting plate assembly
5 Contact plate
6 Bulb holder
7 Bulb holder interior
8 Seating ring
9 Securing screw
12 Speed nut
11 Headlamp bulb (not UK)
12 Sidelamp bulb
13 Lens unit
14 Bulb retainer
15 Mounting plate assembly
16 Adaptor
17 Bulb (not UK)
18 Bulb holder interior
19 Seating ring
20 Securing screw
21 Speed nut
22 Flasher bulb
23 Bulb holder interior
24 Flasher lens
25 Screw
26 Gasket
27 Nut
28 Lockwasher
29 Bulb/flasher
30 Tail/stop bulb
31 Lens & reflector assembly
32 Gasket
33 Screw
34 Retainer strip
35 Gasket
36 Bulb holder stop/tail
37 Bulb holder flasher
38 Nut
39 Washer
40 Cover
41 Nut
42 Washer
43 Stop lamp switch
44 Retaining nut
45 Roof lamp assembly
46 Roof lamp assembly
47 Festoon bulb
48 Lens
49 Lens
50 Screw
51 Door switch – interior light
52 Screw
53 Luggage boot lamp assembly
54 Bulb
55 Clip
56 Clip
57 Bracket
58 Screw

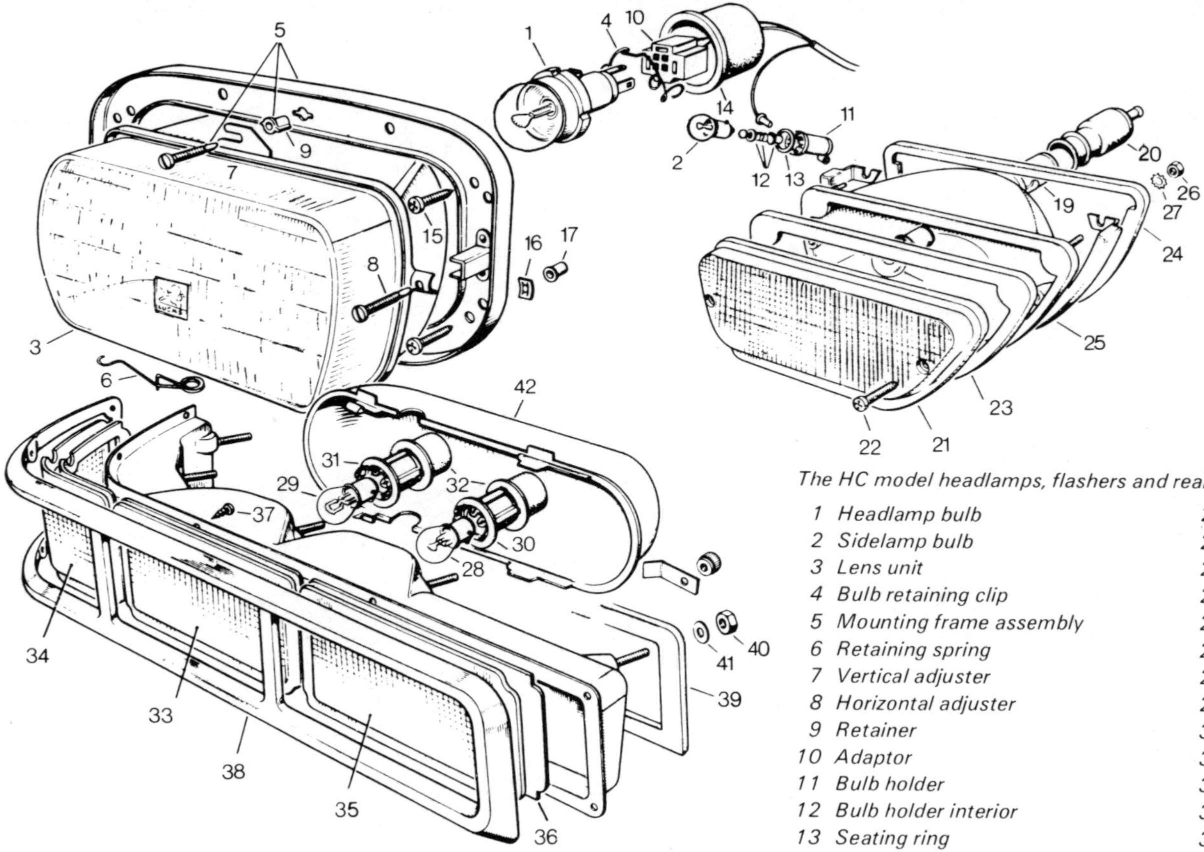

The HC model headlamps, flashers and rear lamp clusters – components

1 Headlamp bulb
2 Sidelamp bulb
3 Lens unit
4 Bulb retaining clip
5 Mounting frame assembly
6 Retaining spring
7 Vertical adjuster
8 Horizontal adjuster
9 Retainer
10 Adaptor
11 Bulb holder
12 Bulb holder interior
13 Seating ring
14 Boot
15 Screw
16 Captive nut
17 Protector
18 Front flasher bulb
19 Bulb holder
20 Grommet
21 Amber lens
22 Lens screw
23 Seal
24 Seal
25 Moulding
26 Nut
27 Lockwasher
28 Flasher bulb
29 Rear lamp and stop bulb
30 Holder – flasher bulb
31 Holder – lamp/stop bulb
32 Dust cover
33 Flasher lens
34 Tail/stop lamp lens
35 Reflector lens
36 Lens seal
37 Screw
38 Bezel
39 Seal
40 Nut
41 Washer

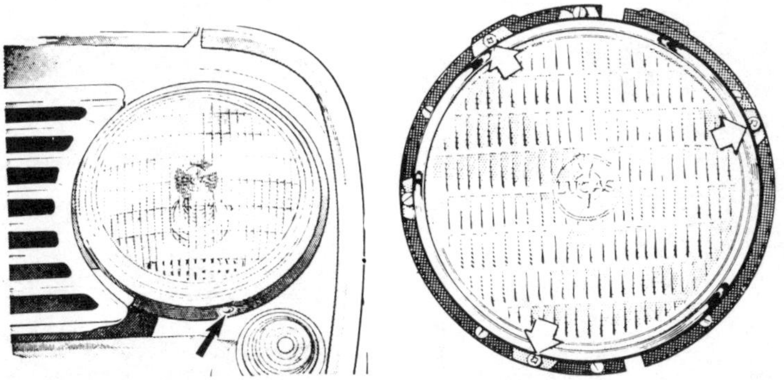

The HA model headlight fixture screws

Pulling off the headlamp connector block

Headlamp bulb removal

bulb-holder free from the headlamp body, then take out the bulb.

HB and HC Series

Access to the headlamps is via the engine compartment. The rear of each headlamp has a rubber shroud which is pulled back to reveal the connection block. Pull off this connector, prise free the bulb retaining clips and withdraw the bulb. The headlight reflectors also contain the side light bulbs – access to these is as described for HA models (above).

Front indicators – bulb removal

The front indicator bulbs are housed in the amber lenses under front bumper in the lower wing. Access to the bulb for removal is made by unscrewing the lens retaining screws and removing the lens. When refitting the lens ensure that it's located correctly with the gasket (which must be in good condition). Don't overtighten the retaining screws or you'll be renewing the lens as well since they crack easily.

Rear combination lights - bulb removal

The stop, tail and indicator bulbs at the rear are incorporated in a single housing on each side, and access to the connectors and bulbs is from inside the boot. Remove the cover and pull out the snap-in-bulbholder and bulb as required, but note that the stop/tail light bulb's a bayonet pin fitting, so make sure the offset pins of the new bulb go in the correct way round (the stop light must be brighter than the tail light when operated).

On estate models it's necessary to remove the body trim pad, which is held by three screws, before you can get at the lights.

Sidelight bulb removal

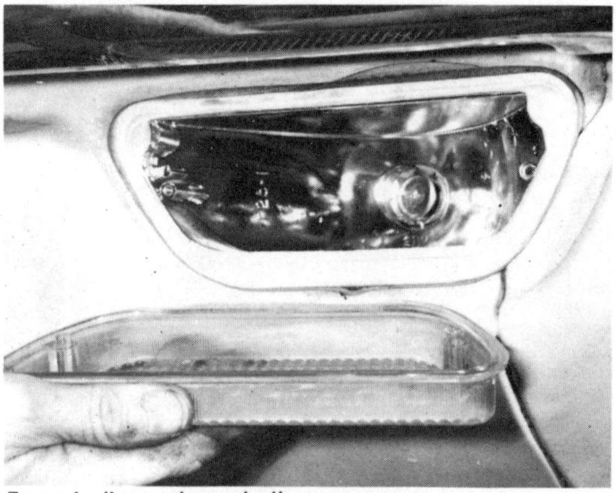

Front indicator lamp bulb access

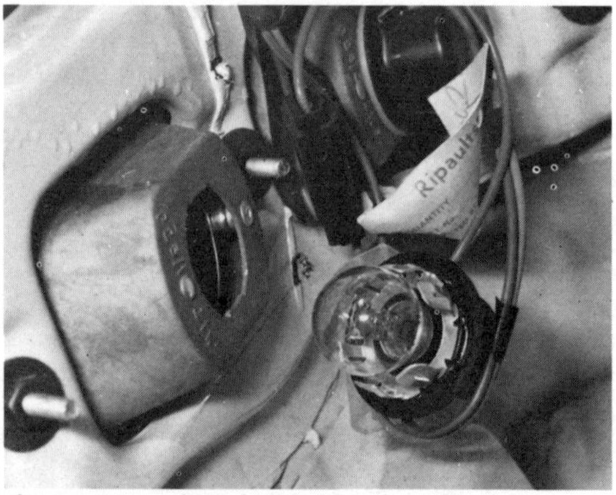

Access to rear lamp bulbholders from boot

Rear number plate lamp lens removed

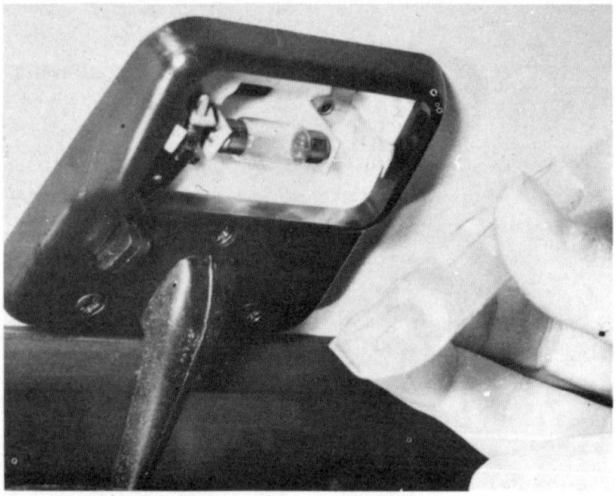

Interior lamp bulb access on HC Viva

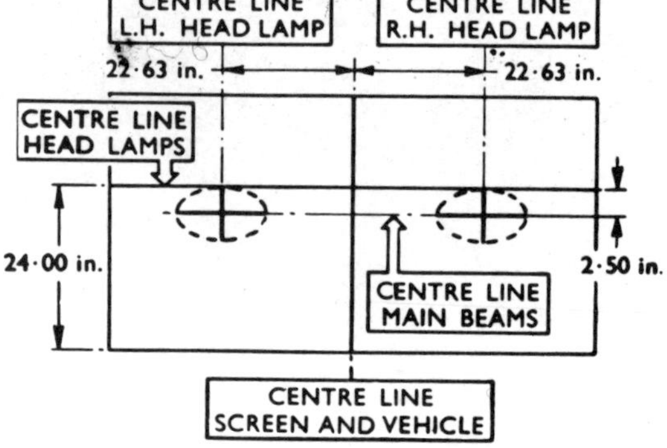

The headlight beam adjustment

Number plate light

The number plate light bulb can be removed after undoing the hood lens retaining screws in the rear bumper.

Headlamp beam adjustment

The headlamp beam alignment is something which rarely alters and is best set using proper optical equipment. Lamps which don't dip correctly are illegal, and if it's obvious that yours need attention, don't delay. If the lamps are seriously misaligned, temporary adjustment can be made by turning the adjuster screws. To reach these, first remove the headlamp moulding and, with the vehicle facing a vertical wall at a distance of 25 feet, set the beams as shown in the drawing.

Spares and repairs kit

The tool kit supplied with the car is the minimum necessary to change a wheel, and nothing more, so should a breakdown occur, you may well be thankful for a basic tool and spare parts kit of your own. Obviously it's not practical to motor around carrying vast quantities of spare parts and a full range of mechanic's tools, but a few of the items more likely to be needed, and easily used at the roadside, can get you out of a spot of bother. Apart from a selection of tools (these are discussed in Tools For the Job) the sort of things you should consider carrying are:

Spark plug - correctly gapped and clean.
A length of HT lead sufficient to reach from the distributor to the furthest plug.
A fan belt (see below).
Distributor rotor arm, set of points and condenser.
Roll of insulating tape.
A torch, or extension light and lead with crocodile clips.
A container of spare coolant.
Fuses.
Breakdown warning triangle.
Windscreen de-icer and scraper.
Hand cleaner and rags.
Your Haynes Handbook and/or Owner's Workshop Manual.

The list could of course be expanded indefinitely – for example, you might like to have a set of spare cooling system hoses instead of just a hose bandage.It's up to you to decide what you're likely to use in a roadside situation.

So far as the fan belt's concerned, it's worth mentioning that you can buy an emergency type which doesn't require any bolts to be loosened to fit it, and which will suit a wide variety of cars. With one of these in the car, you can get on your way quickly and fit a proper replacement belt at your leisure.

Another item well worth carrying is an aerosol can of ignition water proofer such as 'Damp-Start', which is particularly beneficial on damp mornings or when motorway spray and rain get into your ignition system. If the car fails to start or misfires under these conditions, a quick squirt applied to the coil, ignition leads and distributor cap will chase off any moisture present and save much time and aggravation drying and cleaning the various individual components.

Emergency windscreen

If you're unfortunate enough to have a broken windscreen, it can not only be a 'shattering' experience but the rest of your journey (or at least until you can get a replacement installed) will be somewhat draughty and possibly wet. Many people who have suffered this experience now carry a spare emergency plastic screen which makes an excellent temporary substitute, and since it rolls up easily, can be stowed in the boot when not in use.

Save It!

Not too unnaturally these days, most people are constantly seeking new ways of saving money and the motorist is certainly no exception. Look, for instance, at the long line of cars outside the garage selling cut-price petrol. Having topped right up to the brim, many drivers will then speed off down the road gleefully thinking they've saved themselves a small fortune, whilst at the rear end the petrol tank overflow pipe's working overtime getting rid of the excess fuel – some saving! Many people's idea of economy motoring seems to start and finish at the petrol pump. They forget about all the other things that contribute to economical motoring, like a correctly tuned engine, and good driving habits.

If the engine's not serviced occasionally it will deteriorate over a period and eventually become unreliable. To work efficiently the engine must first of all be in good general condition, and secondly it must be in good time, which means that the sparking plugs, distributor contact points, carburettor and valve timing components must be in good condition and correctly adjusted.

When these items are allowed to get out of adjustment, the engine suffers from lack of power and the driver's right foot will invariably try to make up for this loss. Any 'saving' made by ignoring the servicing schedules is then paid for indirectly by more frequent visits to the petrol pumps!

Talking of the right foot, this can be, and is with many people, the villain of the piece when it comes to economy motoring. Over-acceleration, staying in the lower gears longer than is necessary, and excessive use of the brakes all contribute to higher running costs. These things are often done subconsciously, so check your driving habits next time you're out in the car.

Leaving the choke out too long is another human error that can be rectified and of course the handbrake must be fully released! High speed cornering may be fun to some, but it greatly reduces the life of tyres, wheel bearings and suspension.

Over the years there have been many economy gadgets produced, all promising instant miracles with the minimum of effort to fit. Sad to relate, the vast majority are little more than a gimmick, at best theoretically brilliant but leaving much to be desired when fitted.

If you're thinking of fitting an economy device, it can only be assumed that your car isn't giving you the miles per gallon you originally expected when you bought it. Before you lash out with your hard-earned cash, first check that the engine's in good condition and that the necessary adjustments have been made correctly.

If you've recently had your engine reconditioned and are positive that it's adjusted correctly, and yet you still get poor consumption figures, it may be that the carburettor's badly worn or damaged. Your money would therefore be far better spent on having the existing carburettor checked and reconditioned by a carburettor specialist or Vauxhall dealer than on a dubious gadget.

The distributor and coil are other likely trouble spots for poor economy. To get a complete check and

Smiths Industries 'Milemiser'

diagnosis, take your car to a tuning specialist who has the necessary knowledge, and perhaps electronic diagnosis equipment, to pinpoint a trouble spot in a relatively short time, and you'll soon recover your outlay in cheaper running costs.

One 'economy device' (to use the term in its widest sense) which *can* repay its cost quite quickly is a vacuum or engine performance gauge, such as the 'Milemiser' from Smiths Industries. This enables a constant check to be kept on the engine's operating range and the idea is to keep the needle in the 'good' sector as much as possible – indicating optimum efficiency and therefore minimum fuel consumption. One of these devices will quickly reveal just how important your own right foot is in the fuel economy game!

Fuel

Your car's designed to run on a particular grade of fuel (star rating). Don't buy fuel that's of a higher rating than this, because you're wasting your money. On the other hand, if you buy a lower rating fuel your engine performance (and probably your engine too) will suffer. If you *are* forced to buy inferior fuel, drive carefully until you can get the correct grade; in these circumstances it's also beneficial to retard the ignition by a couple of degrees, but you've got the bother of resetting it again later.

Tyres

Without any doubt whatever, a radial ply tyre will give you much better value for money than a crossply because, although it will cost a bit more to buy, it will last a great deal longer. Remould tyres can give good service, but they have their limitations when used for family motoring; remould radials now have a more reliable reputation than they had when they first appeared on the market, but sometimes give a bit of trouble when trying to balance them.

So, what have we learnt so far, only that in the broadest terms the more you pay for your tyres, the better value for money you'll get. If you want the best in roadholding *and* tyre life, buy radials; If you want good tyre life but aren't quite so worried about roadholding under adverse conditions, buy crossplies; If you want a good runabout tyre, and aren't thinking of high speeds or long journeys, buy radial remoulds but remember they may give a bit of steering wheel 'shimmy' if used on the front; If you want the cheapest tyre which still complies with the law in safety standards, buy remould crossplies.

Regraded tyres are sometimes available (they used to be known as remould quality or RQ); these are tyres which may have the very slightest of defects in the tread pattern or moulding, but are otherwise perfect. If you get the chance to buy these, buy them – to all intents and purposes they're as good as a new tyre.

It's not generally realised that most major tyre manufacturers also produce tyres under a less well known name at a somewhat cheaper price. These are first class buys too – ask any tyre dealer.

Talking of tyre dealers, it's worth mentioning that they're the people to go to if you're intent on saving money (and who isn't these days). Unless there's a 'special offer' going, the most expensive place to get your tyres will normally be your local garage.

Now let's just briefly consider how to make tyres last. First, keep them inflated properly (see *Filling Station Facts* for the correct pressures). Second, drive sensibly (i.e. no race-track starts or cornering). Third, make sure the wheels are balanced properly (a job for a garage or tyre specialist).

Batteries

Next to tyres, batteries are the most commonly found parts sold by specialists. A top quality battery may cost up to three times the price of the cheapest one that'll fit your car.

Once again, price is related to quality, but isn't necessarily directly proportional. A battery with a twelve month guarantee ought to last that long and a little bit more, but batteries always seem to fail at embarrassing or inconvenient times so it's worthwhile getting something a little bit better. Many of the accessory shops and tyre dealers sell good quality batteries with two or three year guarantees. Buy one of these – it'll be worthwhile in the long run and still cost quite a bit less than the dearest ones around. And if you look after it, it'll look after you, too.

Exhaust systems

The average car gets through several exhaust systems in the course of its life, the actual number depending on the sort of journeys for which the car's used (lots of short journeys will mean condensation remaining inside the exhaust system and helping it to rust out more quickly).

The best place to go when your Viva needs a replacement exhaust (or maybe just part of the system) is one of the specialist 'exhaust centres' which have sprung up in recent years. They keep huge stocks to fit most mass-produced cars, and offer free fitting as well as discount prices on the parts themselves. You'll almost certainly show a worthwhile saving compared with getting your Vauxhall dealer to fit the exhaust (which will involve labour charges as well).

If you're planning to keep your car for several years it would certainly be worth thinking about an exhaust system made from stainless steel. It'll normally cost you considerably more than an ordinary

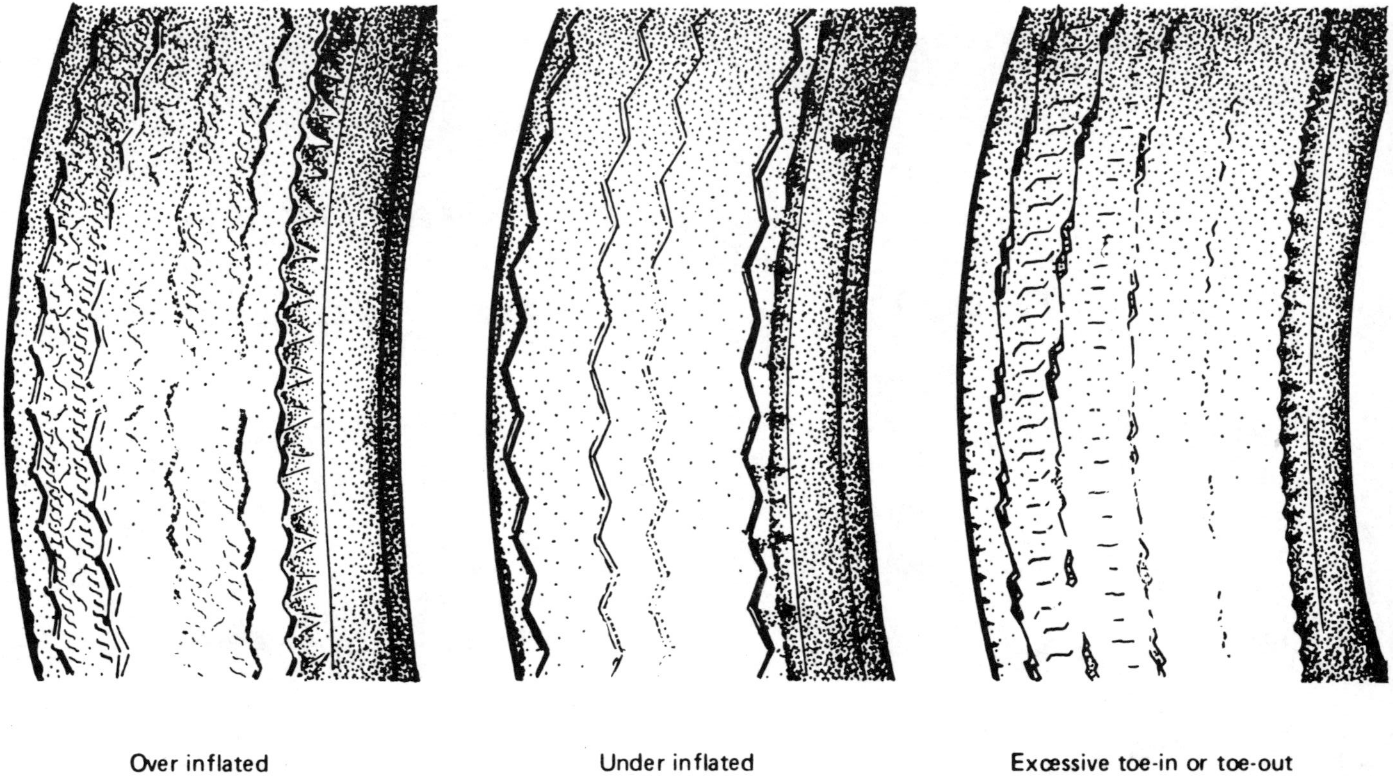

Tyre tread wear patterns

mild steel replacement, but on the other hand should last the remainder of the car's life. If you're interested, talk it over with one of the exhaust specialists – they're usually stockists of the stainless steel kind too.

Lubricants and the like

Good cheap engine oils are available, but because it's so difficult to find out which cheap ones *are* good, it's safest to stay clear of them. There are plenty of good multigrade engine oils on the market and quite a few are available at sensible prices from the D-I-Y motoring and accessory shops.

Unless circumstances should force you to, don't buy oil in pint or half-litre cans. This is the most expensive way of buying, particularly if it's from a filling station. The big 5-litre (they used to be one gallon) cans are adequate for most purposes, and contain just about the right amount for an engine oil change; an extra can for topping-up between oil changes will probably be required, particularly if your pride and joy happens to be a bit of an oil burner.

Oil is also available in larger drums (which can be fitted with a tap) sometimes at an even bigger price saving. A telephone call or visit to nearby wholesalers may well prove worthwhile.

Antifreeze is always cheaper if you go to the motoring shops, but bulk buying doesn't normally apply because you never need to buy it in any real quantity.

As for greases, brake fluid, etc, you'll never need large quantities – just make sure you buy something that's good quality.

Roof racks

The ever-faithful roof rack has proved a boon to so many motorists, for the extra holiday luggage, but how often do you see cars being driven around with an empty roof rack still attached. Many estimates have been made of the increase in fuel consumption caused by a roof rack, due to wind resistance, and the generally accepted figure is around 10%; with a loaded rack, this figure can be as high as 30%. The moral, then, is obvious, don't use a roof rack unless you have to, and always remove it when it's not in use.

Insurance

Like some of the other things that we've discussed, the service you're going to get from your insurance company will be related to the cost of the cover obtained. A cheap policy's good until you need to make a claim, and then the sort of snags you're going to come across are 'How do I get hold of an assessor to inspect the damage?' or 'How will it affect my No Claims Bonus?'

There are one or two legitimate ways of reducing the policy premium, perhaps by insuring for 'owner driver only', 'two named drivers', or an agreement to pay the first £20 or so of any claim. Many large companies have a discount scheme for their employees if they use the same insurance company; this also applies to bank and Civil Service employees. You may also get a better bargain by insuring through one of the Motoring Associations if you're a member.

What it all adds up to is: (1) Insure well; (2) See what you can get in the way of discounts; and (3) Find out exactly what you're covered for.

Buying spare parts

Apart from the oils and greases which you're going to need, it won't be long before you have to buy a few bits and pieces to keep things running smoothly. Please do remember to clean up any parts which are traded-in on an exchange basis (e.g. brake shoes) and, wherever possible, check that any replacement parts look the same as the old one, either by direct comparison if this can be done, or by reference to any of the illustrations in the appropriate Section of this book.

Spare parts and accessories are available from many sources, but the following should act as a good guide when they're required.

Officially appointed Vauxhall/Bedford garages

Although these dealers should be able to supply just about everything for your car, it's generally true to say that the prices may be higher than you *need* pay.

Other garages

In recent years the big British car manufacturers have introduced a replacement parts scheme whereby they market parts for each others' cars under trade names such as Mopar, Unipart and Motorcraft. Though you'll pay the same sort of prices for any of these parts ranges, you may well find that your local Chrysler or Ford dealer can supply you with guaranteed parts for your Vauxhall or Bedford, and that can't be a bad thing.

Accessory shops

These are usually the best places to get items like contact breaker points, oil filters, brake shoes and pads, spark plugs, light bulbs, fan belts, lubricants, touch-up paints etc. – the very things you're going to need for the general servicing of the car. They also sell general accessories and charge lower prices but, what's equally important, they have convenient opening hours and can often be found not too far from home.

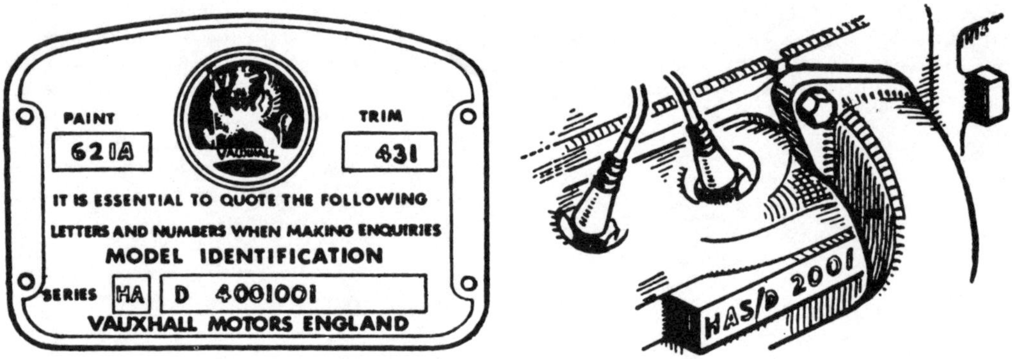

The HA model identification plate and engine number plate

Motor factors

Good factors will stock all the more important components of the engine, gearbox, suspension and braking systems, and often provide guaranteed parts on an exchange basis. They're particularly useful to the more advanced do-it-yourself motorist.

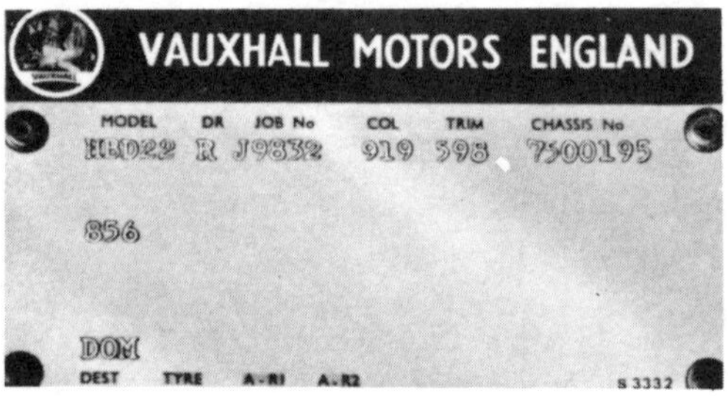

The HB model identification plate . . .

. . . and engine number plate.

Vehicle identification numbers

Before undertaking any service or repair tasks on your Viva, we recommend that you read through the relevant instructions to see just what's involved and what parts are likely to need replacing.

If you know in advance which items are to be renewed, they can be bought or ordered beforehand thus saving time and trouble. It may be of course that the offending assembly will have to be dismantled before you can decide which parts need to be renewed.

Whatever the case, when ordering spare parts, it's always helpful and sometimes essential that the vehicle identification numbers (engine number and chassis number) are quoted. You may have intended to make a note of these before but not got around to it – if this is the case, note them now – in your diary perhaps, or inside the cover of this Handbook.

The Viva has been in production for some years now and in the interest of continuous improvement various modifications have been made. It therefore follows that not all similar-looking components are interchangeable and the exact model, year and identification numbers should therefore be quoted to obtain the correct replacement. Where possible, take the old part along and compare it with the new.

Location of identification numbers

HA models

The identification number's stamped on a plate located on the left-hand side of the bulkhead in the

Vehicle identification plate (HC Viva)

engine compartment. The respective models are marked as follows:

HAS	*2 door Standard Saloon*
HAD	*2 door De Luxe Saloon*
HAD21	*2 door De Luxe 90 Saloon*
HAH	*2 door SL Saloon*
HAA21	*2 door, SL90 Saloon*
HAE	*6 cwt/HA110 Van*
HAV	*8 cwt/HA130 Van and Beagle*

HB models

From August 1966 to July 1967 the model and chassis numbers were stamped on a plate inside the engine compartment mounted on the battery support bracket. After that date a plate bearing a new numerical identification code will be found on the left-hand front door pillar. The two different methods of identification can be summarised as follows:

Old Code	New Code	Model
HBS	93111	Standard Saloon
HBD*	93311	De Luxe Saloon – 2 door
–	93369	De Luxe Saloon – 4 door
HBH*	93511	SL Saloon – 2 door
–	93569	SL Saloon – 4 door
–	93711	GT Saloon
HBW	93315	De Luxe Estate Car
HBG*	93515	SL Estate Car

**The suffix '21' after these codes indicates the SL90 model.*

HC models

Two identification plates are fitted; one is mounted on the top of the instrument panel on the left and can be read through the windscreen. The other gives additional information of the paint colour and production options in code form and is fitted on the right-hand wheel arch panel in front of the battery, under the bonnet. The numbers given in the 'New code' column (above) for the HB continue to apply to the equivalent models in the HC range.

Location of engine numbers

For all models the engine number will be found stamped on the right-hand side of the engine (as seen from the driver's seat) just below No. 1 (the front) spark plug.

Vital Statistics

You're going to need to know a lot of the information set out here that's applicable to your particular model, at some time or other, even if it's only to win a bet in the pub! Let's go in head first then, starting with the engine.

ENGINE	**HA**	**HB**	**HB/HC**
No. of cylinders	4	4	4
Firing order	1-3-4-2	1-3-4-2	1-3-4-2
Cubic capacity	1057 cc (64.5 cu in)	1159 cc (70.7 cu in)	1256 cc (76.6 cu in)
Bore	74.3 mm (2.925 in)	77.7 mm (3.062 in)	81 mm (3.188 in)
Stroke	60.96 mm (2.40 in)	60.96 mm (2.40 in)	61 mm (2.40in)
Gross BHP			
Low compression engine (7.3 : 1	47.8	52.5	58.5
CR) at (rpm)	5200	5400	5400
Standard engine (8.5 : 1 CR)	50.1	56.2	62.5
at (rpm)	5200	5400	5400
Extra performance engine (9.0 : 1	60.1	68.9	—
CR) at (rpm)	5400	5800	—

Valve clearances (hot)

HA 1057 cc	0.010 in (0.254 mm) exhaust
HB/HC 1159 cc	0.006 in (0.152 mm) inlet
HB/HC 1159 cc (extra performance engine)	Inlet and exhaust 0.008 in (0.203 mm)
HC 1256 cc	Inlet and exhaust 0.008 in (0.203 mm)

Ignition system

Spark plugs:	
Type (all models)	AC 42 XLS or equivalent.
Gap: Later 1256 cc engines with emission control air cleaner	0.040 in (1.016 mm)
All other engines	0.030 in (0.762 mm)
Distributor:	
Type (all models)	Delco-Remy D202 (automatic centrifugal advance)
Contact points gap (all models)	0.019 in (0.482 mm) to 0.021 in (0.533 mm)
Static ignition timing:	
All 1057 cc and 1159 cc except high compression	$4\frac{1}{2}°$ BTDC

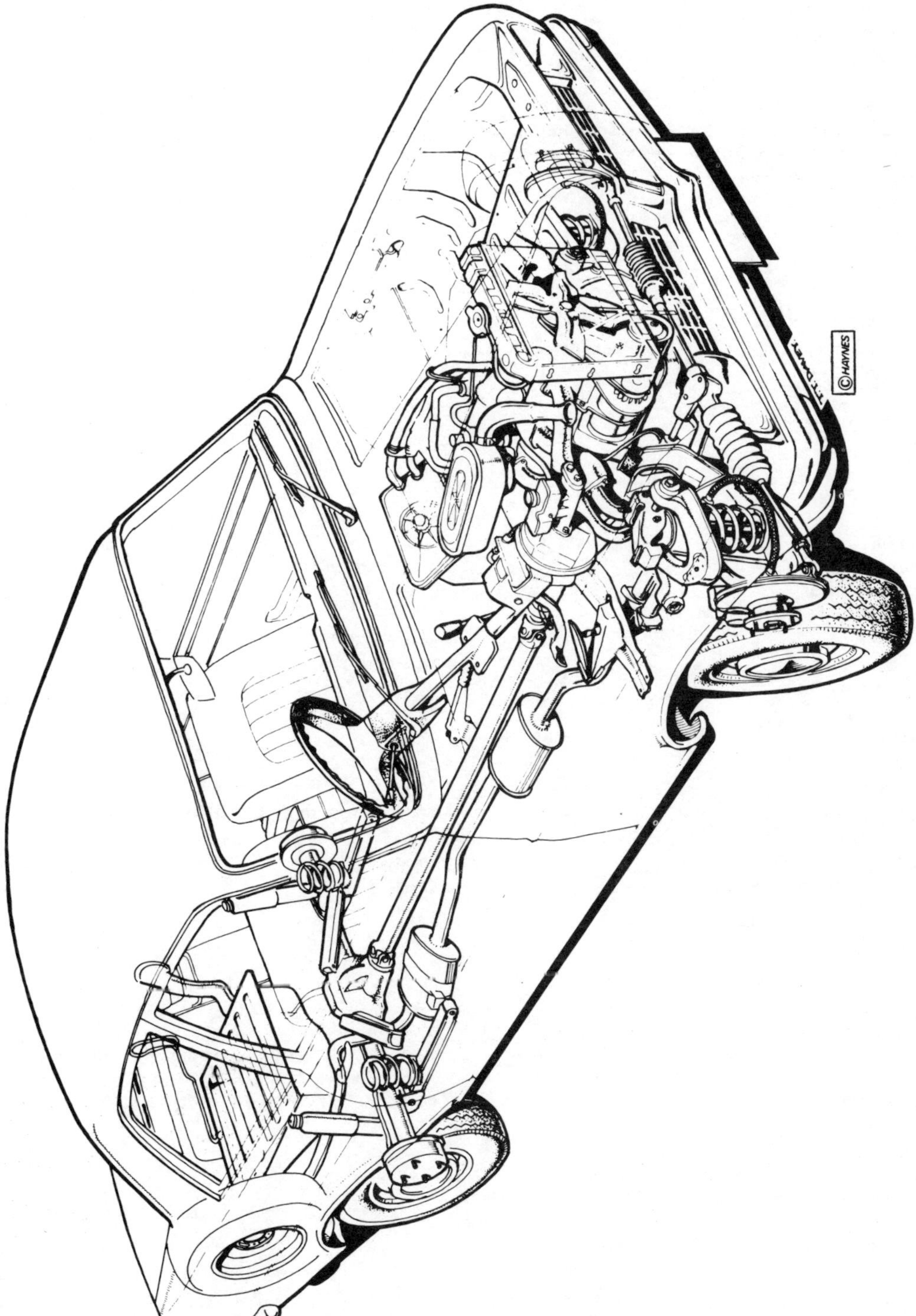

Cutaway drawing of the Viva HC

1159 cc high compression	9° BTDC
All 1256 cc	9° BTDC

Cooling system

Pressurised thermo-syphon with fan belt driven impeller pump. A thermostat controls coolant temperature in the engine block. The radiator cap incorporates a pressure and vacuum relief valve.

Radiator cap blow-off pressure	
HA/HB models	$6\frac{1}{4}$ to $7\frac{3}{4}$ psi
HC models	$13\frac{1}{2}$ to $17\frac{1}{2}$ psi
Fan belt tension	Depression of $\frac{1}{2}$ in under 9 lbs pressure between the generator and fan pulleys.

Fuel system

AC mechanical fuel pump actuated by an eccentric on the camshaft.

Fuel octane requirement	98 (9.0 : 1 CR) 97 (8.5 : 1 CR) 90 (7.3 : 1 CR)
Carburettor	
HA models	
Fixed choke type	Solex B30 PSE 1
Variable choke type	Stromberg 150 CD
HB (except 9.0 : 1 CR)	
Fixed choke types	Solex B30 PSE1 – 6 Zenith 30 IZ
HB (9.0 : 1 CR)	
Variable choke	Zenith/Stromberg 150 CDS
HC (1159 cc)	
Standard	Zenith 301Z
High performance	Zenith/Stromberg 150 CDS – 3350
Automatic transmission models	Zenith/Stromberg 150 CDST – 3352
HC (1256 cc)	
Standard	Zenith 301Z
Automatic transmission models	Zenith 34 IVET

TRANSMISSION

Clutch

Make	Borg and Beck or Laycock
Type	Single–plate, diaphragm spring, operated mechanically by cable.
Cable adjustment	$\frac{1}{4}$ inch free play between cable end and operating lever

Gearbox

Manual, four forward speeds and reverse, with synchromesh on all forward gears

Ratios	**Saloon**	**Estate**
1st	3.765 : 1	3.461 : 1
2nd	2.213 : 1	2.213 : 1
3rd	1.404 : 1	1.404 : 1
4th	1 : 1	1 : 1
Reverse	3.707 : 1	3.707 : 1

Rear axle

Semi-floating, live with hypoid bevel pinion	
Ratio (standard)	4.125 : 1
Ratio (optional)	3.89 : 1

Overall gear ratios

These can be calculated as follows:
Gear ratio X rear axle ratio = overall gear ratio

STEERING AND SUSPENSION

Type	Rack and pinion
HA models	
Ratio	(to September 1964) 18 : 1 (September 1964 on) 16 : 1
Steering wheel turns (lock to lock)	(to September 1964) 3.79 (September 1964 on) 3.14
Turning circle	29 ft
HB models	
Ratio	15.5 : 1
Steering wheel turns (lock to lock)	3.2
Turning circle	31.5 feet
HC models	
Ratio	16.3 : 1
Steering wheel turns (lock to lock)	3.16
Turning circle	32.2 ft (9.62 m)

Steering geometry

HA models	
Front wheel alignment	0.08 in to 0.14 in toe in
Camber angle	$\frac{1}{4}$° to 1°
King pin (steering pivot) inclination	7° to 8°
Castor angle	$\frac{1}{4}$° to 3°
HB models	
Front wheel alignment	Parallel to 1.045 in
Camber angle	0° to 2° 30′ positive (or 1° 45′ neg to 0° 45′ positive after chassis nos DE339003/OV252007)
King pin (steering pivot) inclination	5° 38′ to 8° 38′ (or 7° 10′ to 10° 10′ after chassis numbers as above)
Castor angle	2° 0′ to 4° 30′ (each side to be within 1° of other side)
HC models	
Front wheel alignment	0.04 in toe in to 0.05 in toe out
Camber angle	2° negative to 0°
King pin (steering pivot) inclination	7° 55′ to 10° 25′
Castor angle	2° 30′ to 4°

Front suspension

HA models

Independent, double wishbone with transverse leaf spring and telescopic hydraulic dampers mounted vertically through the upper wishbone.

HB and HC models

Independent, double wishbone with coil springs and telescopic hydraulic shock absorbers inside the springs.

Rear suspension

HA models

Semi-elliptic leaf springs mounted on bodyframe side rails on rubber bushed pins and shackles. Special spring to axle mountings with an additional crossmember to support the downward stresses on the pinion extension. Two telescopic hydraulic dampers are mounted at an angle from the spring seats to brackets on the underframe.

HB and HC models
Coil springs, with rear axle located by two longitudinal and two radius arms. Two telescopic shock absorbers are mounted apart from the springs.

Wheels and tyres

HA and HB models	
Wheels: steel disc, 4 stud fixing	4J x 12 inch
Standard tyres fitted:	
Saloons with standard engines	5.50 – 12 4 ply
Saloons with '90' engines and all estate models	6.25 – 12 4 ply low profile
HC models	
Wheels: steel disc, 4 stud fixing	4J or $4\frac{1}{2}$J x 13 inch
Standard tyres:	
Standard and De Luxe saloons	5.20 x 13 4 ply
De Luxe Estate and all SL models	6.25 x 13 4 ply
Optional	165/70HR–13 radials
Revised range 1976:	All except Viva E have 155 SR-13 radials

Tyre pressures
See *Filling Station Facts*

BRAKES

On Standard and De Luxe models, hydraulically operated drum brakes are fitted on all four wheels, the front having two leading shoes. All 90 and HC SL models have disc brakes fitted to the front wheels and servo power assistance to the hydraulic system. On HC models the hydraulic master cylinder is dual so that the circuits for the front and rear brakes are independent. This safety feature provides partial braking in the event of a loss of pressure in one place, and eliminates total failure. The handbrake operates the shoes of the rear brakes independently of the footbrake, through a mechanical linkage of wire cables and levers.

ELECTRICAL SYSTEM

Battery

HA models	
Voltage	12V positive earth (early models) or negative earth.
Capacity	32 amp hour at 20-hour rate
HB and HC models (negative earth)	
Standard 12V	Exide 6VTA 7BR or Lucas BH7/9A 32 amp hour at 20 hour rate
Heavy duty 12V	Exide VTM 11 BR 53 amp hour at 20 hour rate

Light bulbs

HA models	
Headlamps (rhd) (early models)	60/45W (sealed beam)
Headlamps (rhd) (later models)	45/40W (pre focus)
Headlamps (lhd)	50/40W or 45/40W (pre-focus)
Parking and front flasher	6/21W small bayonet cap
Tail and stop	6/21W small bayonet cap
Rear flasher	21W single centre contact
Rear number plate	6W miniature centre contact
Interior light	10W festoon
Flasher warning	2.2W miniature centre contact
Instruments and warning lamps	2.2W miniature centre contact

HB models

Headlamps (rhd)	60/50 watt – bayonet fitting
Headlamps (lhd)	45/40 watt – clip fitting
Side, number plate, and boot interior lamps	6 watt – miniature centre contact
Tail/stop lamp	6/21 watt – small bayonet cap
Direction indicator lamps	21 watt – single centre contact
Interior	6 watt – festoon
Direction indicator, main beam indicator, ignition and oil warning and instrument lamps	2.2 watt – miniature Edison screw

HC models

Headlamps (rhd)	Duplo D filament 45/40W. Asymmetric dip. Unified European cap
Headlamps (lhd)	Double filament 45/40W. Unified European cap
Side, number plate and boot	6W miniature centre contact
Tail and stop	Double filament 5/21 watt. SBC (offset pin) cap
Flashers	21W single centre contact
Instrument panel	3W wedge base, capless
Ignition warning	3W wedge base, capless
Other warning	1.5W wedge base, capless
Interior	6W festoon

Fuses

The fuse unit is located in the engine compartment on the scuttle panel. Fuse ratings are as follows:

HA models	4 x 25 amp fuses
HB and HC models	4 x 35 amp fuses with provision for two spares

CAPACITIES

	HA	HB and HC 1159 cc engines	1256 cc engines
Petrol tank	7 gal (31.8 litres)	8 gal (36.4 litres)	8 gal (36.4 litres)
Cooling system (with heater)	11.25 pints (6.39 litres)	10.2 pints (5.80 litres)	10.2 pints (5.80 litres)
Cooling system (excl. heater)	10.25 pints (5.82 litres)	9.2 pints (5.23 litres)	9.2 pints (5.23 litres)
Engine sump (dry engine)	5.5 pints (3.13 litres)	5.5 pints (3.13 litres)	5.5 pints (3.13 litres)
Sump refill	4.5 pints (2.55 litres)	4.5 pints (2.55 litres)	4.5 pints (2.55 litres)
Sump refill (plus filter change)	5.0 pints (2.84 litres)	5.0 pints (2.84 litres)	5.0 pints (2.84 litres)
Gearbox	1.0 pint (0.517 litre)	0.9 pint (0.51 litre)	0.9 pint (0.51 litre)
Rear axle	1.25 pints (0.71 litre)	1.25 pints (0.71 litre)	1.25 pints (0.71 litre)

DIMENSIONS AND WEIGHTS

	HA	HB	HC
Wheelbase	91.5 in (2324 mm)	95.8 in (2433 mm)	97 in (2464 mm)
Track			
Front	47.4 in (1203 mm)	51.0 in (1295 mm)	51.4 in (1316 mm)

Rear	48.2 in (1224 mm)	51.0 in (1295 mm)	51.5 in (1318 mm)
Overall width	59.4 in (1509 mm)	63.0 in (1600 mm)	64.7 in (1643 mm)
Overall height			
Saloon	53.3 in (1354 mm)	53.1 in (1349 mm)	53.1 in (1349 mm)
Estate	57.4 in (1458 mm) (van)	53.4 in (1356 mm)	53.4 in (1356 mm)
Overall length			
Saloon	155.1 in (3940 mm)	161.2 in (4094 mm)	162.8 in (4135 mm)
Estate	150.2 in (3815 mm) (van)	160.4 in (4074 mm)	162.0 in (4115 mm)
Ground clearance	4.7 in (119 mm)	5.0 in (127 mm)	5.0 in (127 mm)

Kerb weights

HA models	
Viva Saloon	1564 lb (709 kg)
Viva De Luxe Saloon	1585 lb (719 kg)
Viva SL Saloon	1612 lb (731 kg)
Viva De Luxe 90	1601 lb (727 kg)
Viva SL 90	1631 lb (740 kg)
Van HA 110	1654 lb (749 kg)
Van HA 130	1706 lb (774 kg)
Beagle	1680 lb (760 kg)

HB & HC models	**HB***	**HC****
Saloon (2-dr)	1704 lb (773 kg)	1764 lb (800 kg)
Saloon de Luxe (2-dr)	1740 lb (789 kg)	1800 lb (817 kg)
Saloon de Luxe (4-dr)	1780 lb (807 kg)	1840 lb (834 kg)
Saloon 'SL' (2-dr)	1765 lb (901 kg)	1896 lb (860 kg)
Saloon 'SL' (4-dr)	1805 lb (819 kg)	1936 lb (878 kg)
Estate de Luxe	1878 lb (852 kg)	1890 lb (857 kg)
Estate 'SL'	1892 lb (858 kg)	1990 lb (903 kg)
Saloon 'SL 90' (2-dr)	1793 lb (814 kg)	1852 lb (840 kg)
Saloon 'SL 90' (4-dr)	1833 lb (832 kg)	1892 lb (858 kg)
Estate 'SL 90'	1920 lb (871 kg)	1946 lb (883 kg)

* Add 64 lb (29 kg) for Borg-Warner automatic transmission
** Add 46 lb (21 kg) for GM automatic transmission.

Tools for the Job

For anyone intending to tackle car servicing, a selection of good down-to-earth tools is a basic requirement. The initial outlay, even though it may appear to be something approaching the national defence budget,could well be less than the labour charges for one full service on top of this, you should be paying less for the oil and replacement parts by getting them yourself so, provided you've two or three hours to spare, you must be on to a winner.

A small but important point when buying tools is the quality. You don't have to buy the very best in the shop but, on the other hand, the cheapest probably aren't much good. Have a word with the manager or proprietor if you're in doubt; he'll tell you what's good value for money.

It's very difficult to tell you exactly what you're going to need, but the list below should be a help in building up a good tool kit. Combination spanners (ring one end, open-ended the other) are recommended because, although more expensive than double open-ended ones, they give the advantages of both types.

Combination spanners to cover the range $\frac{1}{4}$ to 1 in AF
Adjustable spanner – 9 inch
Spark plug spanner (with rubber insert)
Spark plug gap adjustment tool
Set of feeler gauges
Brake adjuster spanner ($\frac{1}{4}$ in AF, square)
Screwdriver – 4 in blade x in dia (plain)
Screwdriver – 4 in blade x $\frac{1}{4}$ in dia (crosshead)
Pliers – 6 inch
Junior hacksaw
Tyre pump
Tyre pressure gauge
Grease gun
Oil can
Fine emery cloth or oilstone
Wire brush (small)
Funnel (medium size)
Hydraulic jack or strong screw type
Pair of axle stands (concrete or wooden blocks will do it you're careful about choosing them)
Hose brush

Additionally you'll need suitable containers to drain the engine gearbox and axle oils into, and also one that can used to wash parts in. An old 1 gallon oil

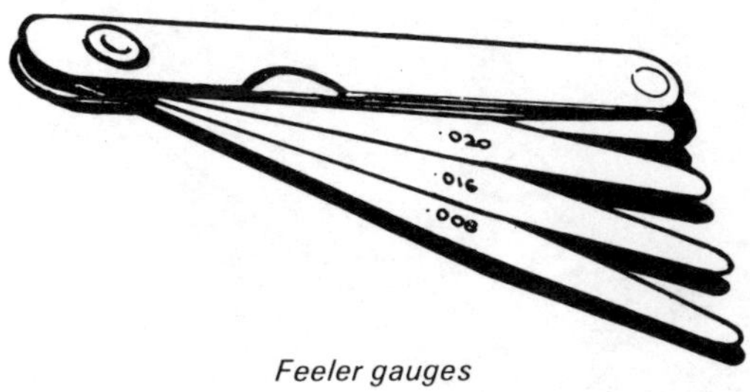

Feeler gauges

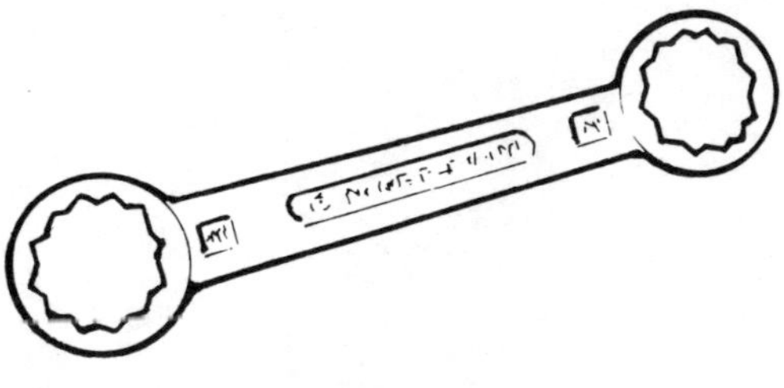

Double-ended ring spanner

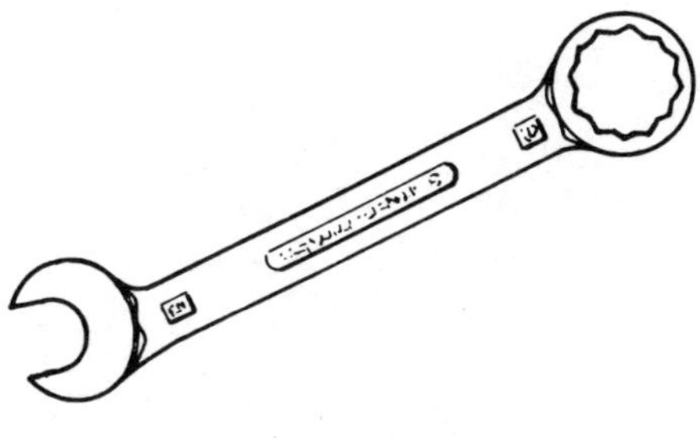

Combination ring/flat spanner

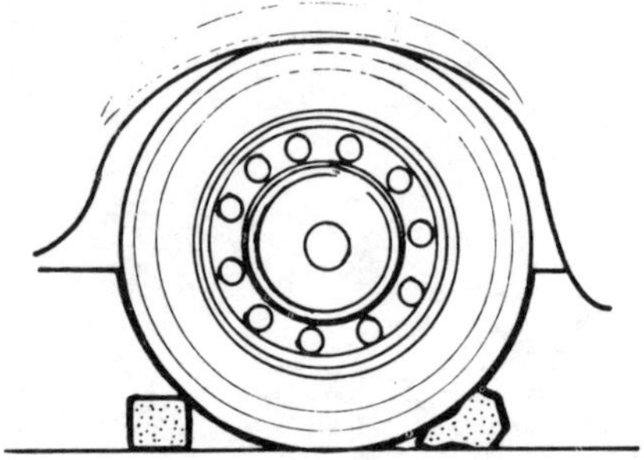

Always wedge the wheels before jacking

Spread the load under the foot of the jack

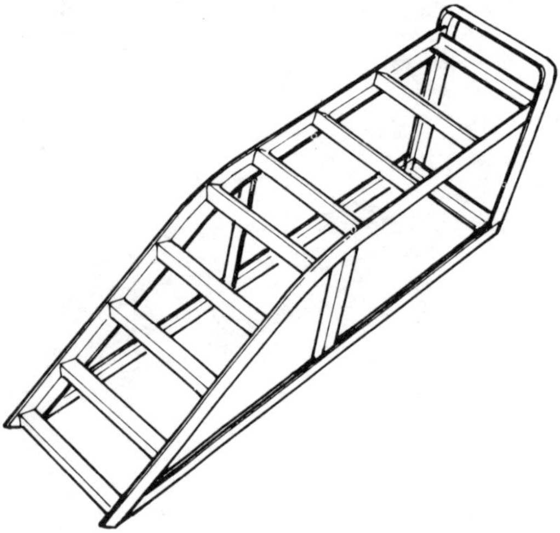

Vehicle ramp

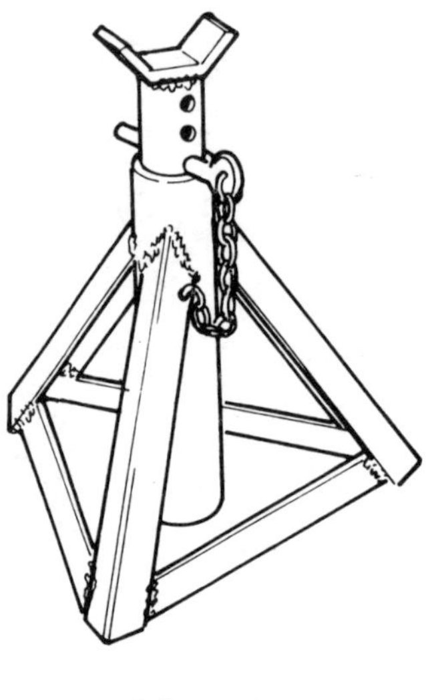

Axle stand

can will do to drain the oil into if you cut a suitable size hole in the side face. An old washing-up bowl's ideal too, and can also be used to clean components off in – but husbands – check with your wife first, she may not have bought a replacement and you don't want any more expense at the moment! Some non-fluffy rags will also be required to clean parts with and to mop up the odd drop of oil spilt. If sawdust's available, keep some handy to soak up any major oil spillage. If you can buy, beg or borrow a boiler suit to work in, this will help to keep you clean and allows greater freedom of movement when working underneath the car.

You may find that a pair of metal ramps is a very useful investment, providing an alternative to the jack or axle stands when you want to get at the underside of the car but don't need to remove the wheel(s). Most ramps available give a lift of between 9 inches and 1 ft and you can, of course, drive either the front or back end of the car on to them – but you'll still need to engage a gear and chock the other two wheels for safety's sake.

Hopefully, your attempts at car servicing are going to show you that it can all be worthwhile, and having worked your way through the various jobs listed in the Service Schedules you'll be able to see that there are many others which can be done without becoming a mechanical wizard. For this purpose, Haynes publish first class Owner's Workshop Manuals for the various Viva models which detail just about every operation that can conceivably be done on these cars. It'll mean buying a few more tools, but to hell with it – you're out to save yourself some money and ;get a good job done in the process.

If and when you do get to this stage, the next items to put on your toolkit shopping list are a good socket spanner set ($\frac{1}{2}$ inch drive, and preferably including a ratchet, extension bar, universal joint and spark plug socket) and a torque wrench for use with the sockets.

While we're talking about tools, it's worth

mentioning some of the tune-up aids that are on the market. A visit to a good motor accessory shop can be an enlightening experience, just to show you the sort of things available. Later in this book, you'll find a bit about 'bolt-on goodies', but all we'll concern ourselves with here are three items.

Stroboscopic timing lamp: The most accurate way of checking ignition timing (that's the time at which the spark occurs) is with the engine running, and for this a stroboscopic (strobe) light is used (take a look at *Car Jargon Explained* if you're lost already). This is connected to No. 1 spark plug lead and the beam is shone on to the crankshaft pulley mark. Any proprietary light is supplied with full connecting and operating instructions.

Dwell angle meter: This is used for measuring the period of time for which the distributor points remain closed during the ignition cycle of one cylinder, and provides a more accurate method of setting-up the ignition than can be done by simply setting the points gap. Dwell angle meters normally incorporate a tachometer (rev counter if you prefer), which can be useful for checking engine idle speed.

Cylinder compression gauge: This is very useful for tracing the cause of a fall-off in engine performance. It consists of a pressure gauge and non-return valve, and is simply screwed into a spark plug hole while the engine is turned over on the starter.

Two other useful items are a hydrometer, which is used for checking the specific gravity of the battery electrolyte (this will tell you if you have a dud cell which won't hold a charge), and a 12-volt lamp on an extension lead with crocodile clips which can be connected to the battery terminals.

Care of your tools

Having bought a reasonable set of tools and equipment, it's the easiest thing in the world to abuse them. After use, always wipe off any dirt and grease using a clean, dry cloth before putting them away. Never leave them lying around after they've been used. A simple rack on the garage wall, for things you don't need to carry in the car, is a good idea. Keep all your spanners and the like in a metal box – you can wrap some rags around them to stop them rattling if you're going to carry them in the boot of the car. Any gauges and meters should be carefully put away so that they don't get damaged or rusty. Do take a little care over maintaining your tools too. Screwdriver blades, for example, inevitably lose their keen edges, and a little timely attention with a file won't go amiss.

Service Scene

If you've read this book so far, you'll be more conversant with your Viva and the various things you'll need to carry out the basic service and maintenance tasks. Hopefully it hasn't put you off too much, so take heart and think of the cash you're going to save compared with the comparatively little effort involved. D-I-Y servicing isn't as difficult or mysterious as you may think ...

However up-to-date the design and engineering of a car may be, it's still important to carry out servicing and inspections at regular intervals to keep the car safe, to prolong its active life, and to maintain a sensible resale value. The old maxim of prevention rather than cure was never truer than in connection with car servicing. Whether it be casting your eagle eye over the general workings of the car or getting down to the service tasks in a workmanlike (or workwomanlike) fashion, it's all going to be worthwhile in the long run. Remember that a worn part won't put itself right and isn't a thing to be lived with. Fix it as soon as you find it, even if it's not time for the next service.

In this Chapter, we've tried to present the servicing tasks in a logical way to minimize the amount of jacking up, etc, which may be a prelude to the actual job. The items listed are basically those recommended by the car manfacturers, but are supplemented by some additional ones which we think are well worth the extra trouble.

If you've recently bought the car, the safest thing is to go right through all the Service Schedules (not on the same day, or course!) unless you can really satisfy yourself that the previous owner was as meticulous about things as you'd like to be. If you don't use the car regularly enough to clock up the scheduled mileage until well after the time interval that's quoted as an alternative guide, always use the time intervals as your basis for servicing. You'll see that we've included Spring and Autumn check-ups, too, just so that you can make sure your car's as fit as possible for the season ahead.

Safety

Accidents do happen, but 99% of them can be prevented by taking a little care. We're going to list a few points which should reduce any accident risk, and we'd like you to read through them before starting work – it could prove to be very worthwhile.

DON'T run the engine in the garage with the doors closed – exhaust fumes are highly poisonous.

DON'T work in an inspection pit with the engine running – the fumes will tend to concentrate at the lowest point.

DO keep long hair, sleeves, ties and the like well clear of any rotating parts when the engine's running.

DON'T grab hold of ignition HT leads when the engine's running – there's just the possibility of an electric shock, particularly if the leads are dirty or wet.

DO chock the rear wheels when jacking up the front of the car, and vice versa. Where possible, also apply the handbrake and engage first or reverse gear.

DON'T rely on the car jack when you're working underneath. Axle stands, or wooden or concrete blocks should be used, to give additional support.

DO wipe up oil or grease from the floor if you spill any (and you will do, sooner or later).

DO get someone to check regularly that everything's OK if you're likely to be spending some time underneath the car.

DON'T use a file or similar tool without a handle. The tang can give you a nasty gash if something goes wrong.

DO make sure when you're using a spanner that it's the right size for the nut and that it's properly fitted before tightening or loosening.

DO brush away any drilling swarf with an old paintbrush – never your fingers.

DON'T allow battery acid or battery terminal corrosion to contact the skin or clothes. If it should happen, wash off immediately with plenty of cold running water.

DON'T rush any job – that's how mistakes are made. If you don't think you'll finish the job in time, do it tomorrow, but try not to make this an excuse for forgetting about it.

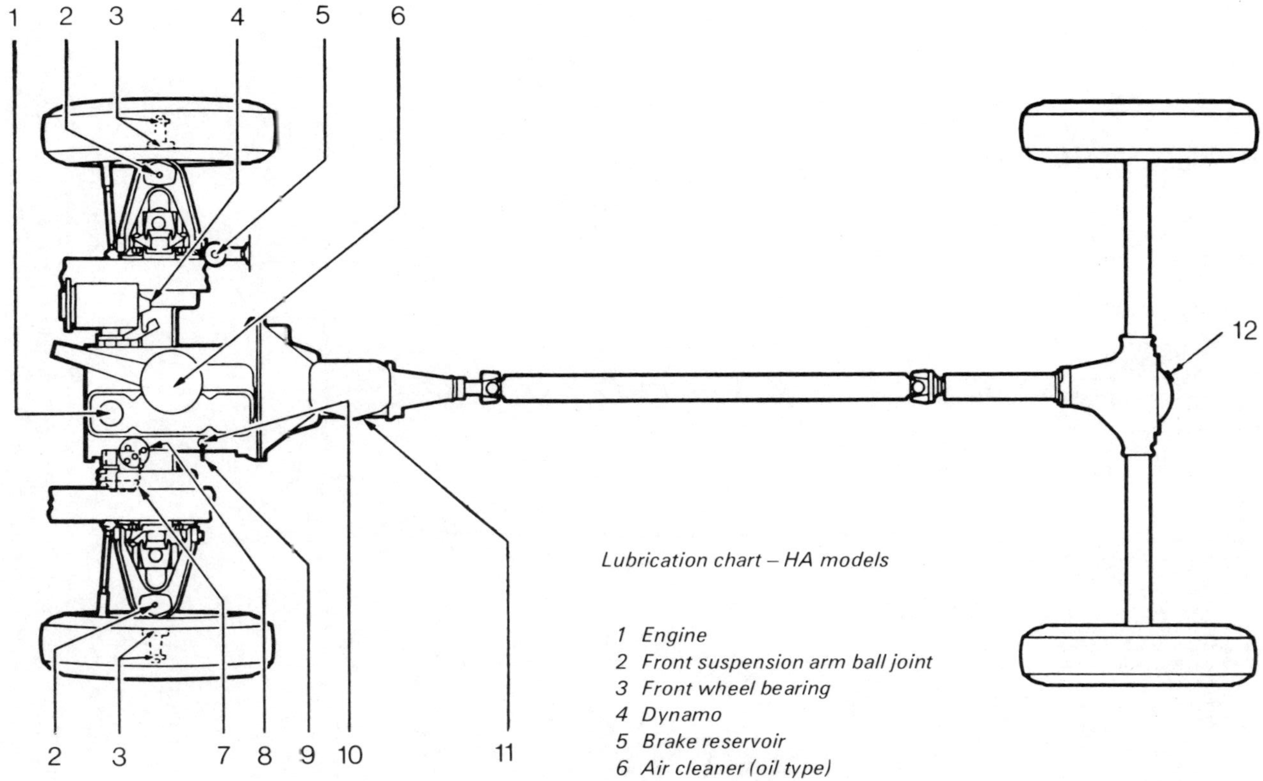

Lubrication chart – HA models

1 Engine
2 Front suspension arm ball joint
3 Front wheel bearing
4 Dynamo
5 Brake reservoir
6 Air cleaner (oil type)
7 Oil filter
8 Distributor
9 Dipstick
10 Crankcase ventilation air cleaner
11 Gearbox
12 Rear axle

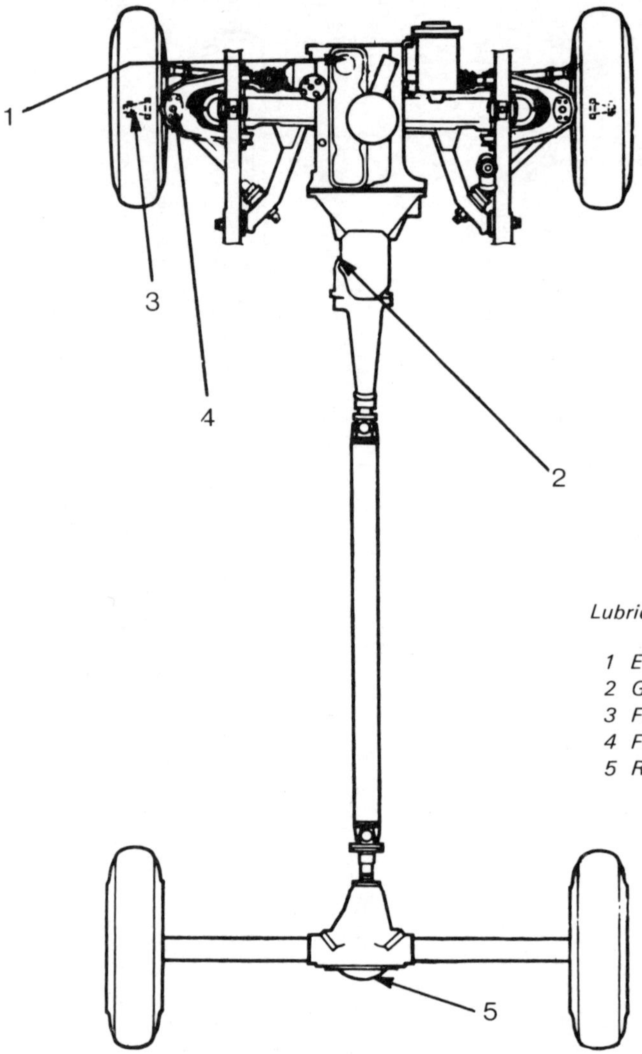

Lubrication chart – HB/HC models

1 Engine
2 Gearbox
3 Front wheel bearings
4 Front suspension arm ball joints
5 Rear axle

DO take care when pouring out brake fluid. If it spills on the paintwork and isn't removed immediately, it'll take the paint off. And do wash your hands well afterwards as it's poisonous.

SERVICE SCHEDULES

Regular maintenance and service checks should be carried out as specified by the manufacturers. If they're ignored, delayed or forgotten then the routine's disrupted, safety reduced, and possibly your expenses increased in the long run.

The time intervals and mileages given are for the average private motorist under normal operating conditions. If the mileage you cover is consistently higher than normal or the operating conditions are more severe than most, then a greater service frequency may be necessary. This, of course, is left to your discretion. Remember that even if nothing apparently needs doing, everything should be checked regularly.

It's a good idea to keep a record of each service, noting the date, mileage and items covered. If you've bought the car second-hand, a complete service and check should be completed as soon as possible. Sometimes a service record is supplied with the car, but it's no guarantee that the work has been carried out as stated.

Removing radiator cap

Engine oil top-up

Battery with filling cover removed

WEEKLY, BEFORE A LONG JOURNEY, OR EVERY 250 MILES

These checks are most easily done when buying petrol.

1 *Check radiator coolant level*

This should preferably be done with the engine cool, but if it's quite hot and the cap has to be removed, first place a good sized cloth over the cap. By doing this you'll prevent any escaping steam and/or boiling water from scalding your hand. When removing the cap turn it *slowly* anticlockwise whilst applying downwards pressure. Don't remove the cap completely until the steam pressure has escaped.

The coolant level in the radiator should be 1 inch (25 mm) below the bottom of the filler neck. If when topping up you overfill it don't worry too much as it'll run out of the overflow pipe until the correct level's obtained.

Before refitting the radiator cap, ensure that the cap seal's clean and in good condition.

If the radiator's filled with antifreeze mixture, then the level must be topped up using a mixture of equal strength. If water only is continually added during topping up, the mixture will be diluted and lose its effective strength. If continuous topping up is necessary, then the fault must be investigated and cured. The most likely cause will be leaky hoses, or hose connections, faulty radiator pressure cap, or leaking radiator. If the fault's not obvious on checking, then get your Vauxhall dealer or local garage to pressure-test the system and put it right as soon as possible.

2 *Check tyre pressures and tread condition*

With the tyres cold, check their pressures, (including the spare). They must be kept at the pressures specified for your model (see *Vital Statistics).* Check the pressures with your own pressure gauge if you have one, as garage gauges are not normally as accurate as they should be.

If any particular tyre shows signs of persistently losing pressure, investigate the cause and get it put right. Check each tyre for signs of excess or irregular wear or damage and replace if necessary.

3 *Check engine oil level*

To check the oil level accurately, the car must be standing on level ground, and if the engine's been running allow it to stand for a couple of minutes to allow the oil to return to the sump. Take out the dipstick and wipe it clean, then push it back in fully. Remove it again and note the level of the oil. It shouldn't be allowed to drop below the 'add oil' mark. If the oil's at that level it will need 2 pints to refill it to the 'full' mark. Don't overfill – this can cause damage. If oil has to be added frequently to keep up the level, you either have a bigger-than-average oil leak or else the engine's tired and due for some treatment.

Use a good quality oil; a multi-grade with anti-corrosion additives such as Castrol GTX is recommended.

4 Check battery electrolyte level

Two types of battery have been fitted as standard – the Exide battery which has a single filler cover, and the Lucas which has a filler plug for each of the cells. When topping up the Exide type, prise the single cover free and if the electrolyte is below the bottom of the filler tube in any of the cells, pour distilled water (free if you top up at your local garage) into the trough until both cell tubes and trough are full. The cover's then replaced and the cells are automatically topped up.

On the Lucas type battery, remove each filler cap in turn and, viewing through the filler hole, note if the electrolyte level's above the separator guard. If the level's below the guard, in any cell, top it up until it's just above. Do not over-fill. Refit each filler cap, and wipe away any spillage.

The need to top up will increase as the battery gets older, but providing it performs its functions satisfactorily there's no cause for concern. Keep the battery terminals clean and smear them with some petroleum jelly. Make sure the terminals are secure, too.

5 Windscreen washer reservoir

Inspect the level of water in the windscreen washer reservoir and top up if necessary. Adding some special windscreen washing liquid will help to get rid of smears, and in winter will help prevent freezing.

EVERY 3 MONTHS OR 3000 MILES

1 Change engine oil (HA and HB models)

In spite of the engine oil filter and carburettor air cleaner, engine oil becomes progressively more contaminated with dirt and impurities and therefore must be regularly changed. To do this you'll need a container to drain the oil into. The car should be standing on level ground and of course you'll have bought a gallon of replacement oil in advance!

Either arrange to change the oil immediately after the car's been used, or else run the engine up to its normal operating temperature, then switch off. This will allow the oil to flow more freely when draining. Place the container under the sump (preferably beneath the drain plug!) and then unscrew the plug, but take care when finally removing it, as the oil will gush forth and you won't be the first person to lubricate his or her elbow with a sleeve full of hot, dirty oil! Allow the sump to drain completely, clean the drain plug before refilling and use a new washer if required. Refit with the correct grade of engine oil to the level marked 'full' on the dipstick, (don't overfill). See *Vital statistics* for quantity of oil required.

2 Check brake fluid level

Wipe the filler cap of the hydraulic reservoir clean, and unscrew it to check the level of brake fluid in the reservoir. When correct the fluid level should be $\frac{1}{4}$ in (6 mm) below the edge of the rim. If topping up's required, use Castrol Girling Crimson brake fluid. If when checked the level's noticeably lower than it should be, then check it again within a week of

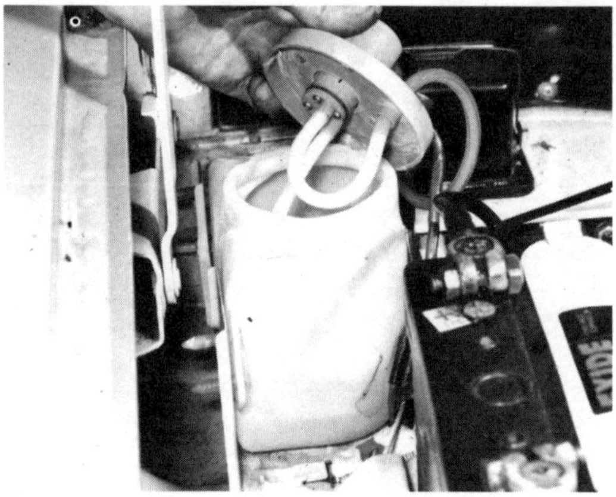

Screenwash reservoir level inspection

Brake hydraulic fluid level check

topping up. If continuous topping up becomes necessary, the brake system will have to be inspected and the fluid leak traced and rectified as soon as possible.

3 *Check condition of brake hydraulic pipes*

A leak in the hydraulic system will render all of the brakes ineffective (with the exception of late models fitted with a dual circuit). Metal pipes lead the fluid to each wheel, and to allow for movement of front and rear suspension, flexible interconnecting pipes are used. The metal pipes will, over a period of time, corrode and regular checks should therefore be made and any suspect pipes renewed before they corrode completely through. Carefully clean the pipes, which are clipped to the bodywork, using a wire brush. Any pipe sections that are pitted, rusty or obviously in poor condition must be renewed without delay – a job for your Vauxhall garage.

The flexible hoses must be cleaned also and twisted and squeezed a little to reveal any cracks or general signs of deterioration. If necessary, renew these as soon as possible too. If when examining the pipes/hoses, an obvious leakage point is discovered, don't use the car any more until the fault's been cured.

4 *Check brake hydraulic wheel cylinder condition*

When examining the pipes of the hydraulic circuit, the respective brake backplates must be inspected at the point where the pipe joins the wheel cylinder, to check that the cylinder seals aren't leaking brake fluid. As oil or grease could also work its way on to the backplate it's essential that you can tell them apart. Hydraulic fluid has a distinctive smell (take off the reservoir filler cap and have a sample sniff to get an indication), and from this it should be possible to distinguish it from anything else.

On disc-braked models, any hydraulic leakage from the wheel cylinder will show at the bottom of the main body of the brake caliper. All hydraulic leaks are dangerous and must be repaired without delay.

5 *Check brake adjustment and wear*

Later HC models are fitted with self-adjusting rear brakes, but on other Vivas covering an average annual mileage under normal conditions, the drum brakes will probably need adjustment every three months at least (the front disc brakes are self-adjusting), and this will be indicated by excessive free play of the brake pedal.

If you're doing an adjustment for the first time it's best to remove the wheel first as the adjusting screws are not very easy to get at. Jack up the car and

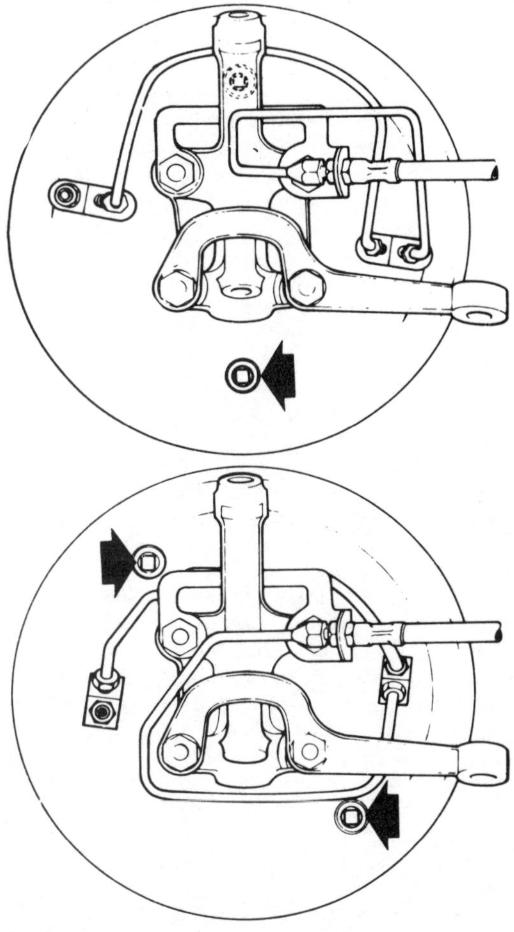

The front backplates: (top) Girling – (bottom) Lockheed. Shoe adjusters arrowed.

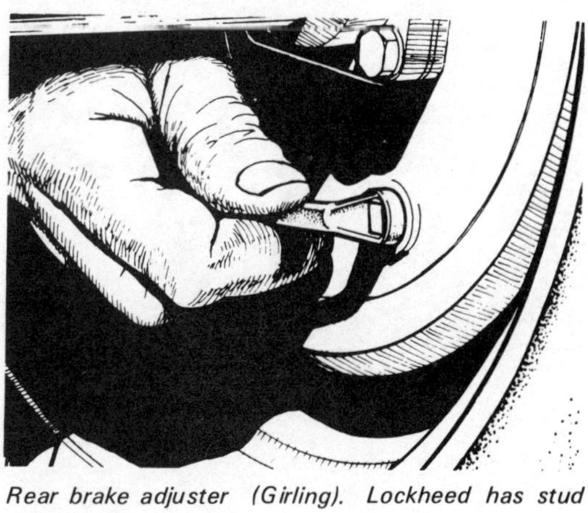

Rear brake adjuster (Girling). Lockheed has stud at bottom.

remove the wheel. For front drum brakes there's an adjusting screw at the top and bottom of the brake backplate. The head of the screw is square and quite small. A proper key spanner should be used to turn it. Anything else is likely to burr the edges, making it more difficult to turn. Often the adjusting screws are stiff due to road dirt and rust; if you have difficulty in moving them, clean them thoroughly, apply some penetrating oil, and leave them for a while.

To adjust the brake shoes, turn the adjuster clockwise until it's impossible to turn the brake drum. Then turn it back one or two notches until the drum's free to rotate once more. Repeat this procedure for the other adjuster. Rear brakes have a single adjuster only at the top of the backplate. Adjustment's the same as for the front brakes.

If brakes are left in need of adjustment for too long a time it's likely that after they're taken up they won't work quite as sharply as they did before, even though they start to operate much sooner. This condition will improve after some use but it may call for futher adjustment. Expect drum brake linings to last approximately twelve months before renewal's required, depending on how and where you drive. Disc pads, whilst needing no actual adjustment, can be examined without difficulty. Remove the wheel and look down into the caliper aperture. The pad consists of a metal backing plate to which friction material's bonded. The friction material should not be less than 0.060 in (1.5 mm) in thickness. If it is, new pads are needed.

If on adjustment of the brakes the pedal free play's still excessive or it feels spongy, then the hydraulic circuit requires bleeding. This job is best entrusted to your Vauxhall dealer or local garage.

6 Check handbrake adjustment

Having adjusted the rear brakes, check that when the handbrake lever's applied, it's fully on after five or six clicks of the ratchet. If the clicks counted are more than this, then the cable adjuster locknut should be slackened and the adjuster tightened to give the correct number of clicks on the handbrake when fully on. If all the thread's been taken up, further adjustment can be made by selecting an alternative pin hole at the brake lever clevis, but if this is necessary either the cable's stretched or the rear brake linings are due for replacement.

7 Check steering linkage and ball joint condition

This check can be made when the car's jacked up at the front for other service checks.

Handbrake linkage lubrication points

Handbrake lubrication point

Checking front wheel bearings for wear

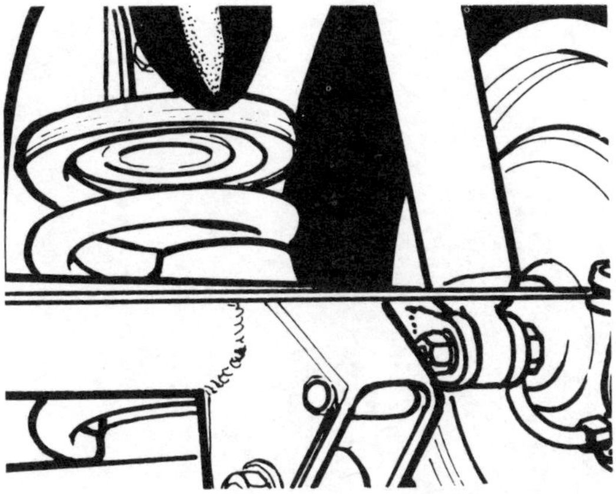

Spring and shock absorber check

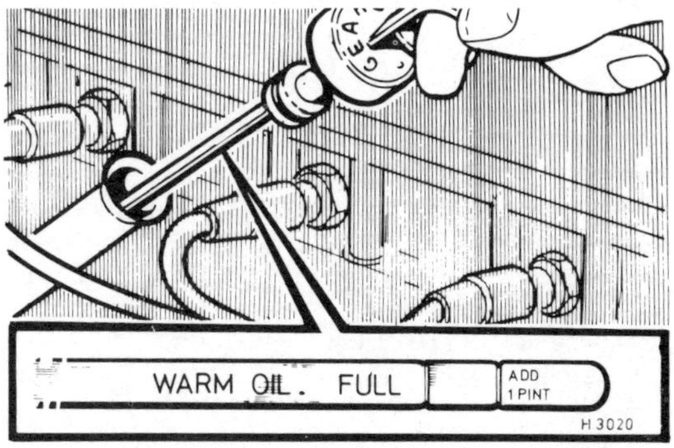

Checking automatic transmission oil level

Assuming that the car's raised at the front with the wheels clear of the ground, grip the tyre with your hands at opposite sides and try to rock it sideways; don't apply too much sustained pressure in any one direction but move it back and forth. There's wear in the linkage if the wheel can be moved to any extent while the steering wheel's stationary.

Inspect the short track rod between the steering arm on the wheel and the steering gear rack, and rock the wheel again. Notice where the play is – probably at the wheel end of the rod in the ball joint. This condition requires renewal of the joint. Repeat the check on the other front wheel. If the play doesn't come from any of the track rod joints the fault must lie in the steering gear, which is more serious. This needs more competant garage attention and could prove a little expensive, but it must be rectified!

Leave the front wheels off the ground ready for the next check

8 Check front wheel hub bearing adjustment

The front wheel hub bearings are of the taper roller type and they must be periodically checked for excessive play which causes hub and wheel slackness. Adjustment of the bearings takes very little time and effort, and if it's left the bearing wear rate will accelerate and affect the steering of the car, as well as causing additional tyre wear.

With the front wheels clear of the ground, grip the top of the tyre with one hand and the bottom with the other and rock the wheel gently. When the bearing's slack it's possible to feel the wheel rocking. There should be no appreciable play, but the wheel must be able to spin freely. However, if you're uncertain or there's an amount of play present, then check and make an adjustment if necessary as follows:

First remove the wheel hub plate. Now prise the hub dust cover free – it can be extracted by tapping lightly with a screwdriver from side to side. With the cap removed, you'll see the bearing retaining nut, spindle washer and split pin. Using a pair of pliers, extract the split pin and remember that a new one will be required on refitting. With a suitable spanner, slacken the nut slightly, then spin the wheel and tighten gradually but not fully. If the nut's overtightened the wheel won't spin freely. If there's a roughness or vibration when the wheel's spun, then the bearing should be removed for examination and renewed if necessary – a job for your garage, or for you with the help of our Owners Workshop Manual. With the nut adjusted to the nearest split pin hole, insert the new split pin and check that the wheel spins freely. Smear some wheel bearing grease into the hub cap and tap it home.

9 Suspension – check springs and shock absorbers

Park the car on level ground, then stand back and admire it! If one corner appears lower than the rest, stop admiring it and take a closer look. The 'droop' could be due to a broken or weak spring or of course a soft tyre. If a spring's broken, or suspected of being a bit frail, have it checked, and renewed if necessary.

To check the shock absorbers, press down on each corner of the car in turn.On releasing the pressure the car should return to its normal height, then stop. If it continues to bounce up and down this indicates that the shock absorber's past its prime and due for replacement.

10 Check automatic transmission fluid level

The transmission fluid should be checked when the engine and transmission are at normal running temperature. The engine should be idling, the drive selector lever at 'P', the car standing level and the handbrake on. The combined dipstick and filler tube's near the bulkhead on the right-hand side of the engine compartment. Clean the top of the tube and pull out the dipstick. Wipe it clean, replace fully and remove it again. Check the fluid level. The distance between the lower and upper marks represents 1 pint of fluid. Add only the recommended transmission fluid such as Castrol TQ 'Dexron' to top up. Under no circumstances use any additives of any sort. Any excessive topping up which may be necessary is unusual and should be investigated further.

11 Examine exhaust system

A leaky exhaust system's inefficient, and if not rectified, can also be dangerous to the driver and passengers on a journey of any length. It must therefore be inspected regularly to see that it's securely attached and free from leaks.

The brackets and hangers under the car which support the exhaust system must all be intact, or additional strain will be put on the rest, eventually causing the system to part company with the car. Have a new bracket fitted if necessary. Pieces of string and wire have often answered the call of duty in an emergency but not for any length of time, so you might just as well do the job properly in the first place where possible.

Temporary repairs can be made to small leaks using a proprietary sealer or bandage, but once you've had to do this, it can be assumed that a new pipe, silencer or system will have to be fitted in the near future.

12 Check lights/indicators and windscreen wipers

To see and be seen at night as well as complying with the law, check that all your lights are in working order, and this of course includes the brake and indicator lights and the hazard warning system if fitted. The ignition will have to be switched on to check the brake and indicator lights, and if you've no assistant handy you can watch for a reflection on a suitable wall or another vehicle. Shop windows are useful for this – try it next time you're parking in the High Street. For replacement of any bulbs that aren't working, see *In An Emergency*.

Check that the timing of the indicators is correct, between 1 and 2 flashes a second. If they are too fast or too slow then the flasher unit's faulty or there's possibly a bad wiring or earth connection to the light on the side in question. If a new flasher unit's to be fitted, ensure that it's handled with care and that the respective wires are connected properly.

Make sure that the windscreen wipers are operating correctly, but not over a dry screen. If the blades on the wipers are scratching or smearing the screen, it's time they were changed.

Exhaust silencer flexible mounting

EVERY 6 MONTHS OR 6000 MILES

(in addition to the 3 months/3000 miles Schedule)

1 Change engine oil on HC models

Under normal conditions HC models can go 6000 miles between oil changes. The procedure's the same as for earlier models whose oil's changed at 3000 miles – refer to that Schedule for the detailed description.

2 Renew engine oil filter element – all models

Assuming that you've drained the engine oil, there will still be some left in the filter, so place the old engine oil container in position under the oil filter. Clean off the outer surface of the filter and the surrounding area of the crankcase. A bolt runs through the centre of the filter and this must be unscrewed to loosen the housing. If the housing sticks in position give it a light tap to dislodge it. Hold the open end up when removing to prevent oil spillage.

Take out the old element from the housing and throw it away. Wash out the inside of the housing with paraffin and remove any sludge, then wipe dry. Note that the spring and plate around the centre bolt are a permanent fixture. Using a small screwdriver, extract the sealing ring from the circular groove in the engine block. Check that the old ring's the same size as the replacement supplied with your new filter before discarding it. Some filters are supplied with two rings, so select the one you require and insert it into the block location groove. Take care that it doesn't get distorted or damaged in any way or it'll leak. Insert the new element into its housing – either way round – and carefully place the housing and element back into position on the block, rotating the

Engine sump drain plug

Location of oil filter

housing against the rubber sealing ring to be sure that it seats correctly. Tighten the retaining bolt securely but don't overtighten.

When the new oil's been added to the engine and it's started up, check that the filter element housing's sealed correctly. If it should leak, stop the engine, loosen the filter retaining bolt and check the oil seal ring for distortion.

3 Clean the crankcase ventilation air filter

On most models there's a cylindrical cartridge which filters the air entering the crankcase, and this is located so that the engine oil dipstick passes through it. Take out the dipstick and unscrew the cartridge, but don't lose the rubber sealing ring. Flush the cartridge clean in paraffin and shake it dry. Using clean engine oil, soak the mesh element, then screw the cartridge back into the block and replace the dipstick.

4 Clean the carburettor air filter (paper element type)

The higher performance '90' series engines are fitted with paper element type carburettor air cleaners, and some standard models also have this type fitted. To clean this type of element, remove the complete air cleaner unit from the carburettor by loosening the retaining clip at the elbow, then prise the cover free by twisting a coin in the groove between the air cleaner cover and body.

Take out the element and clean it by tapping lightly on its end as you rotate it. Accumulation of dust will then fall out. The element must not be brushed cleaned or washed in petrol or any other cleaning fluid.

Clean out the inside of the container and cover

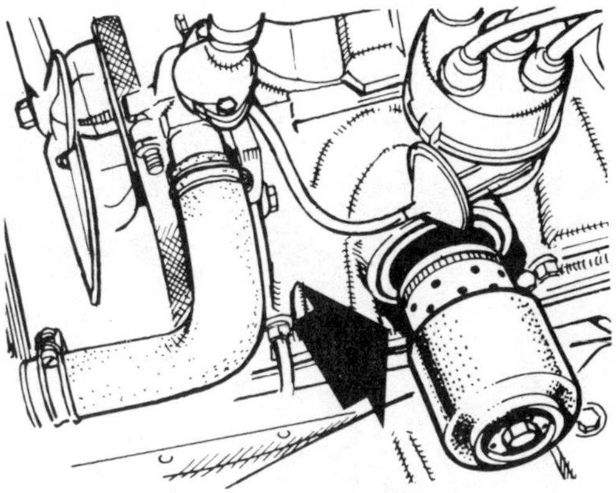

Oil filter replacement

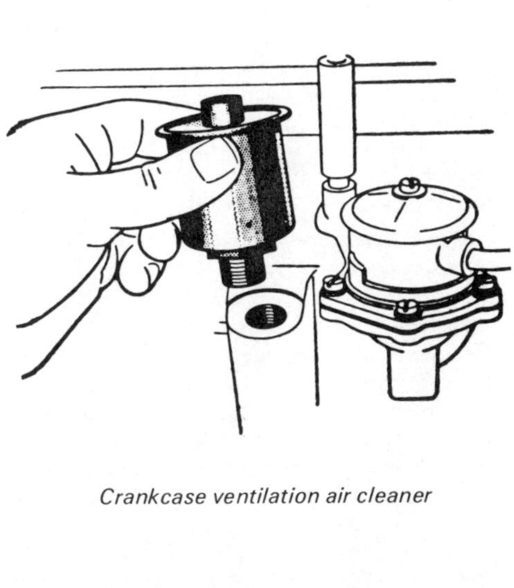

Crankcase ventilation air cleaner

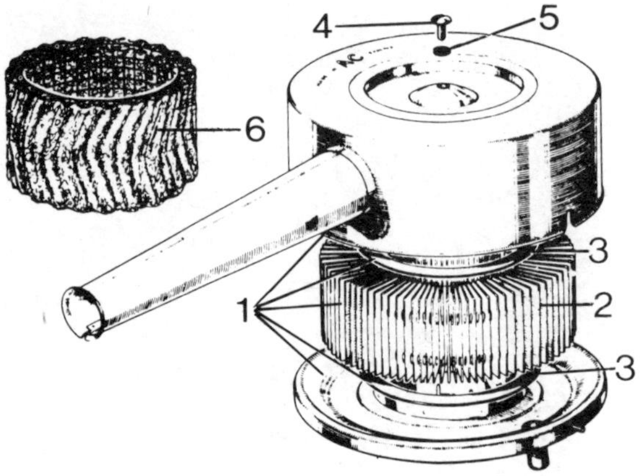

Early type air cleaner showing paper and washable type elements

1 Body and gasket assembly
2 Paper element
3 Gaskets
4 Screw
5 Washer
6 Washable filter element

Removal of air cleaner cover (HC paper element type)

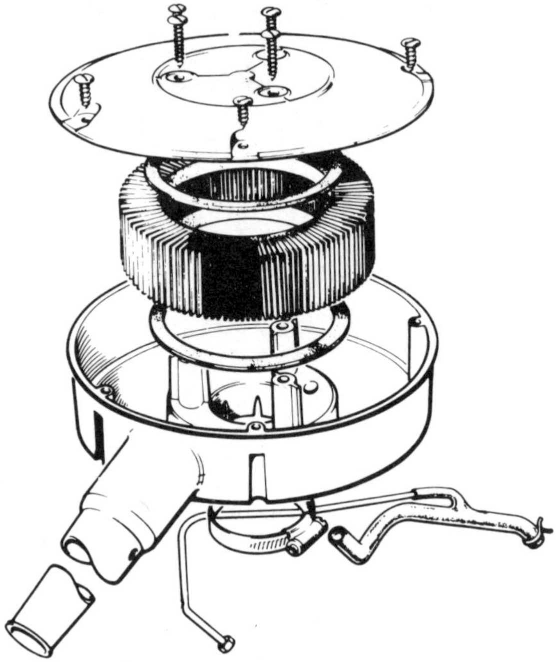

Later type air cleaner

and put back the element, then refit the cleaner unit to the carburettor.

5 Check the carburettor damper oil level (Stromberg carburettor models)

Certain models are fitted with a Stromberg 150 CD variable choke carburettor, which has a movable piston that's hydraulically damped by oil, and this oil level must be checked. To do this, first remove the carburettor air filter unit, but take care not to damage the gasket in between.

On top of the carburettor there's a plastic cap which must now be unscrewed and removed complete with the damper rod. Extract the cap and rod straight upwards to avoid distorting the rod. Put a finger into the air intake aperture in the carburettor and raise the piston so that you can see into its hollow guide rod from above. The rod should contain engine oil to within $\frac{1}{4}$ in (6 mm) of its top. Top up the level if necessary.

Refit the damper rod into the carburettor and note that on some models there's a small collar on the rod which locates into the top of the hollow guide tube of the piston. It's therefore necessary to raise the piston to insert the damper collar, then lower the piston together with the damper and screw home the cap. Now lift the piston again to push the collar fully into the top of the guide tube. To check this, unscrew the cap again sufficiently to view the top of the guide tube. Refit the air cleaner unit.

Solex B30 PSE 1–4 carburettor
as fitted to the HA

1 Strangler flap
2 Flap spindle
3 Return spring
4 Flap screw
5 Needle valve and washer
6 Float arm
7 Arm spindle
8 Float
9 Emulsion tube and correction jet
10 Pump injector
11 Sealing ring
12 Pump release valve
13 Main jet
14 Washer
15 Sealing plug
16 Cam return spring
17 Strangler cam assembly
18 Swivel screws
19 Cam pivot
20 Rod–strangler to throttle, and split pins
21 Distance washer
22 Throttle spindle and pump rod lever assembly
23 Pump diaphragm and spring
24 Throttle floating lever
25 Pump cover screw
26 Pump cover
27 Split pin
28 Pump rod spring
29 Strangler bracket bolt
30 Pump rod
31 Cable clip
32 Rod circlips
33 Strangler bracket
34 Idling mixture volume control screw and spring
35 Gaskets
36 Heat insulator
37 Throttle flap and screw
38 Throttle abutment plate
39 Throttle lever
40 Nut
41 Throttle stop screw and spring
42 Pilot jet
43 Body
44 Gasket
45 Float chamber cover
46 Cover screw

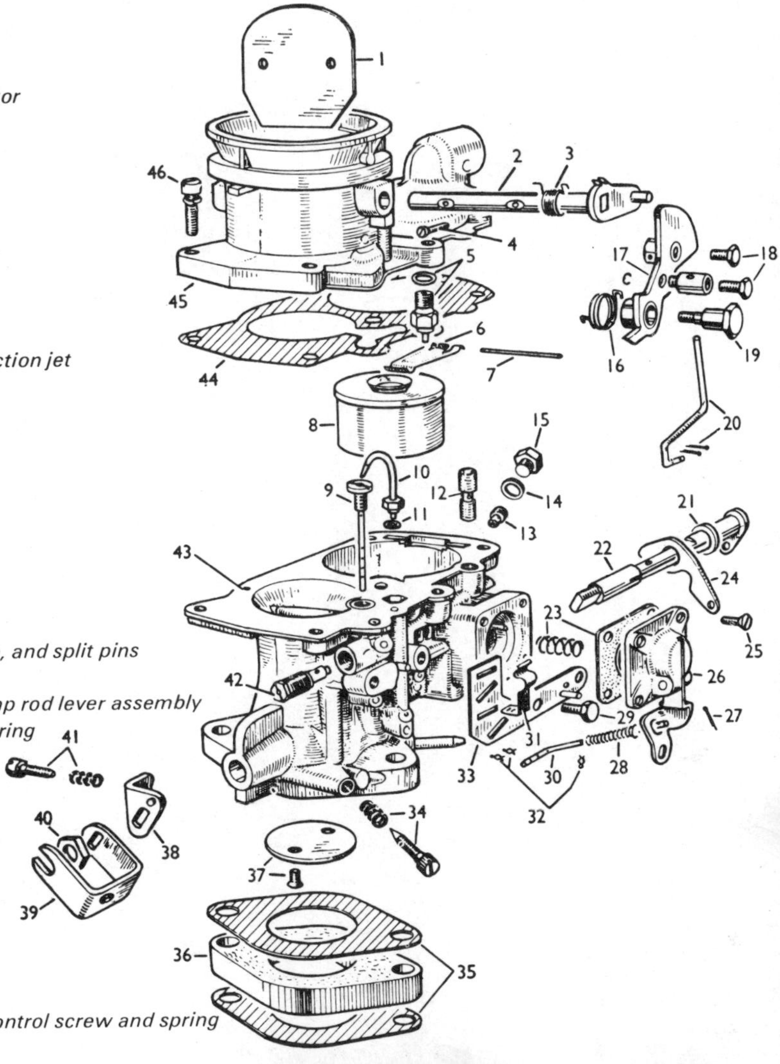

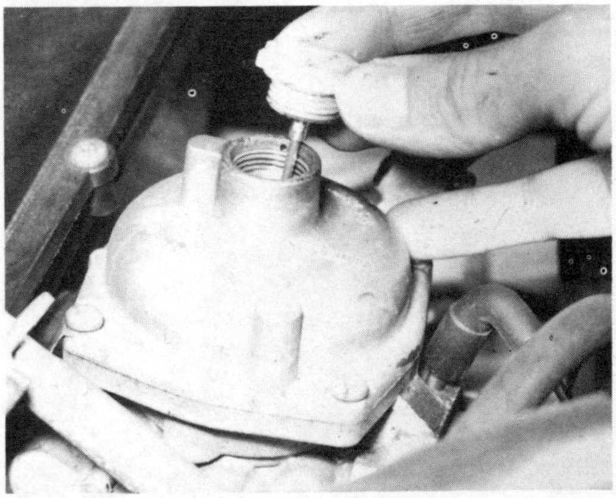

Stromberg Carburettor dashpot level inspection

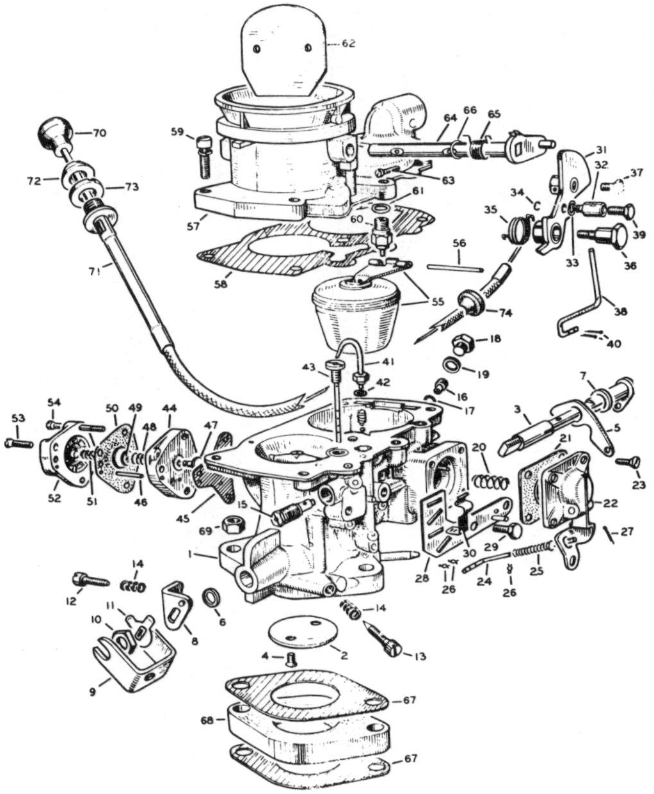

The Solex B30 PSE 1 – 6 and Zenith 3012 carburettors component parts

1 *Body*
2 *Throttle flap*
3 *Throttle spindle and pump rod lever assembly*
4 *Throttle flap screw*
5 *Throttle floating lever*
6 *Distance washer*
7 *Distance washer*
8 *Throttle abutment plate*
9 *Throttle lever*
10 *Nut*
11 *Lockwasher*
12 *Throttle stop screw*
13 *Idling mixture volume control screw*
14 *Spring*
15 *Pilot jet*
16 *Main jet*
17 *Washer*
18 *Sealing plug*
19 *Washer*
20 *Diaphragm spring*
21 *Diaphragm*
22 *Pump cover*
23 *Pump cover screw*
24 *Control rod*
25 *Control rod spring*
26 *Rod circlips*
27 *Split pin*
28 *Strangler bracket*
29 *Bracket bolt*
30 *Cable clip*
31 *Choke cam assembly*
32 *Choke cable anchor lug*
33 *Washer*
34 *Circlip*
35 *Cam return spring*
36 *Cam pivot*
37 *Locking screw*
38 *Link rod*
39 *Choke cable locking screw*
40 *Split pins*
41 *Pump injector*
42 *Sealing ring*
43 *Emulsion tube and correction jet*
44 *Economy unit body*
45 *Gasket*
46 *Vacuum tube*
47 *Valve*
48 *Spring*
49 *Valve washer*
50 *Diaphragm*
51 *Spring*
52 *Economy unit cover*
53 *Screw*
54 *Screw*
55 *Float*
56 *Float spindle*
57 *Float chamber cover*
58 *Gasket*
59 *Cover screw*
60 *Needle valve*
61 *Washer*
62 *Choke flap*
63 *Flap screw*
64 *Flap spindle*
65 *Return spring*
66 *Washer*
67 *Gasket*
68 *Heat insulator*
69 *Carburettor mounting nut*
70 *Choke cable*
71 *Choke cable sleeve*
72 *Locking nut*
73 *Locking ring*
74 *Grommet*

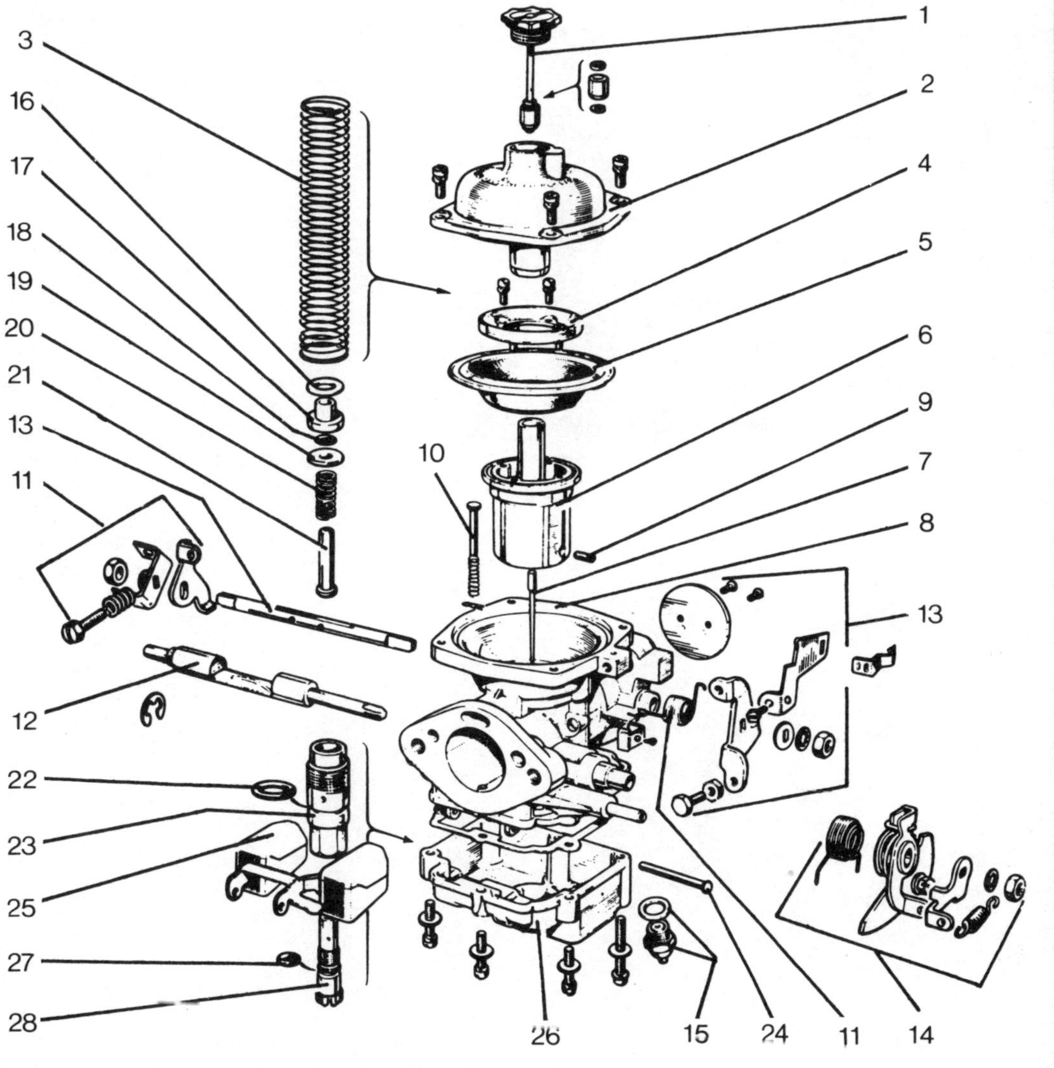

Stromberg 150CD carburettor component parts

1 *Damper*
2 *Suction chamber cover*
3 *Air valve return spring*
4 *Diaphragm retaining ring*
5 *Diaphragm*
6 *Air valve and shaft*
7 *Metering needle*
8 *Main body*
9 *Metering needle locking screw*
10 *Air valve lifting pin*
11 *Throttle stop and return spring assembly*
12 *Starter rod*
13 *Throttle valve and shaft assembly*
14 *Choke cam and lever assembly*
15 *Needle valve and washer*
16 *Washer*
17 *Jet orifice bush*
18 *'O' ring*
19 *Washer*
20 *Spring*
21 *Jet orifice*
22 *'O' ring*
23 *Bushing retainer screw*
24 *Float fulcrum pin*
25 *Float and arm assembly*
26 *Float chamber*
27 *'O' ring*
28 *Orifice adjusting screw*

The mechanical fuel pump

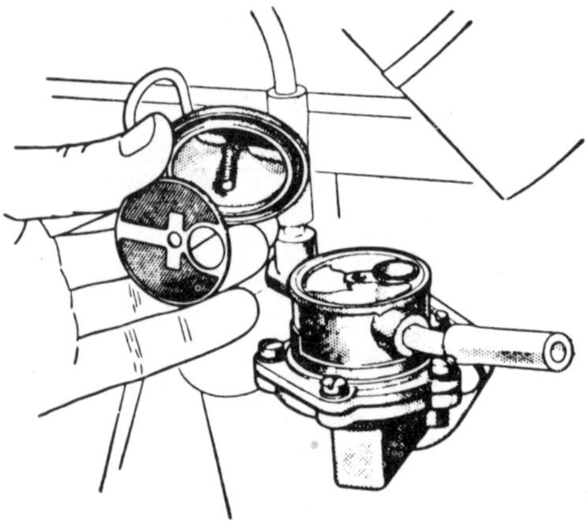

The fuel pump filter

6 *Fuel pump filter*

Note: don't smoke or have any naked lights around when working on the fuel system.

The mechanical fuel pump fitted to all models contains a wire gauze filter screen to prevent any foreign bodies drawn from the fuel tank passing through to the carburettor. The particles of dirt trapped by the gauze must be periodically removed. To do this, first disconnect the input pipe from the fuel pump by pulling it from the input nozzle, and plug the pipe with a pencil or clamp it with a grip wrench to prevent wastage of petrol. Clean off the exterior of the pump. Remove the top cover retaining screw and carefully lift the cover clear, together with the tubular nylon distance piece, sealing ring and gauze filter. The filter can be cleaned in petrol and then blown through to clear the mesh holes. When perfectly clean, replace the filter screen followed by the nylon distance piece and top cover. The sealing ring should be renewed if in doubtful condition. Don't overtighten the cover retaining screw as you may strip the thread and this will cost you a new pump! Reconnect the inlet pipe, then start the engine and check for any signs of leaks.

7 *Clean and reset spark plugs*

It's important that the spark plugs are removed with a proper plug spanner or a box socket of the correct type. When removing or installing the plugs be careful that the spanner/socket's fully located on the plug or it may slip and crack the insulator and your knuckles may suffer in the process too.

Deal with each plug one at a time starting with number 1 (at the front). Pull the HT lead from the plug, and then unscrew and remove it. The condition of the spark plugs the electrodes and indicate your engine's condition and state of tune, as can be seen by the accompanying illustrations. The plugs should be dry at the electrode points and a light tan in colour. If they're oily it suggests a worn engine in need of attention (worn piston rings and/or cylinder bores). The ideal method of cleaning your plugs is to take them along to a garage with a plug cleaning machine which will sand-blast the plug clean and test it under pressure. However, most people get by using wire brush to clean the electrode; wash it clean in petrol and blow dry.

The gap between the central electrode and the horizontal one should be 0.030 in (.75 mm). The gap can be reduced by tapping the horizontal electrode nearer to the centre one. If the gap has to be increased, avoid putting any strain on the central electrode or you may crack the ceramic insulation which surrounds it.

Before replacing the plugs, clean the seats in the engine where they fit, taking great care not to inadvertently push any particles inside the holes.

See that each plug has a sealing washer fitted, and replace the plug firmly but don't overtighten. Wipe the respective plug leads down, also the coil to distributor HT lead.

8 *Check distributor contact breaker points*

A vital component in the car's anatomy, the distributor requires very little attention but when neglected it can cause bad starting and performance. It must therefore receive the regular maintenance it deserves.

To remove the distributor cap, prise the two retaining clips free and lift the cap clear complete with leads. Invert the cap and position it out of the way. Lift off the rotor arm, pulling on the main body – not the spring clip on top. The two contact points are

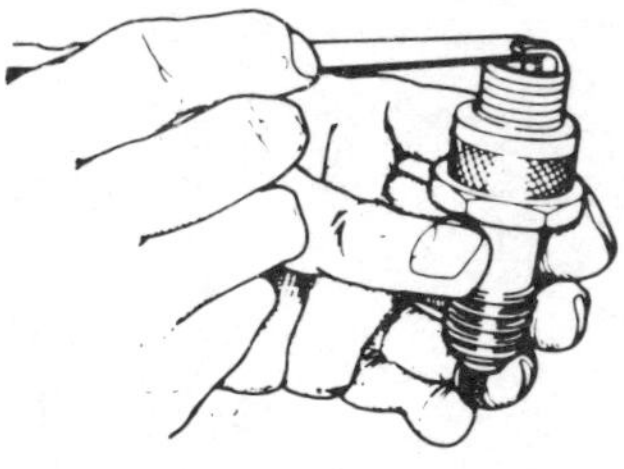

Checking plug gap with feeler gauges

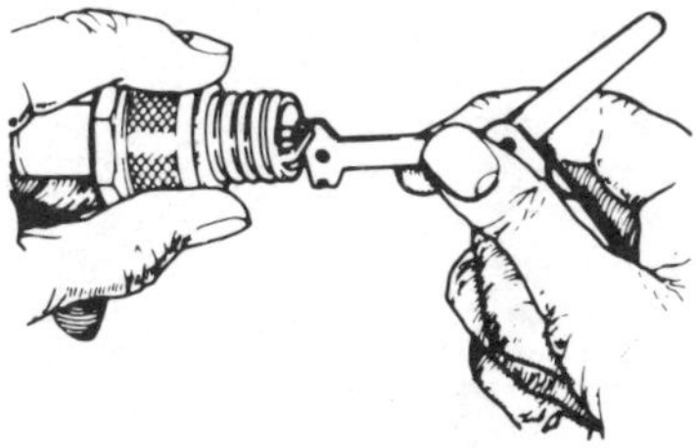

Altering the plug gap. Note use of correct tool.

Spark plug maintenance

White deposits and damaged porcelain insulation indicating overheating

Broken porcelain insulation due to bent central electrode

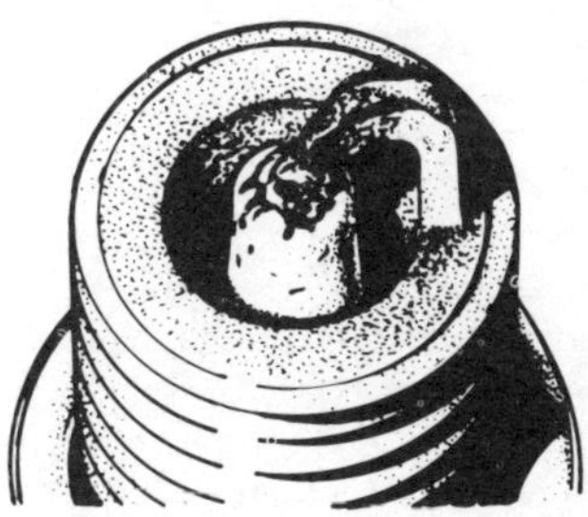

Electrodes burnt away due to wrong heat value or chronic pre-ignition (pinking)

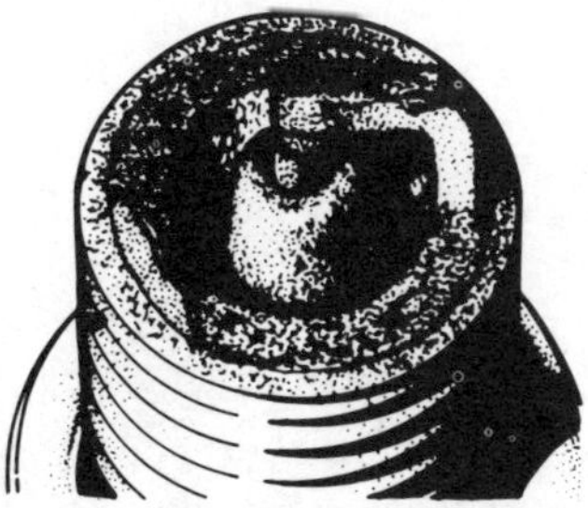

Excessive black deposits caused by over-rich mixture or wrong heat value

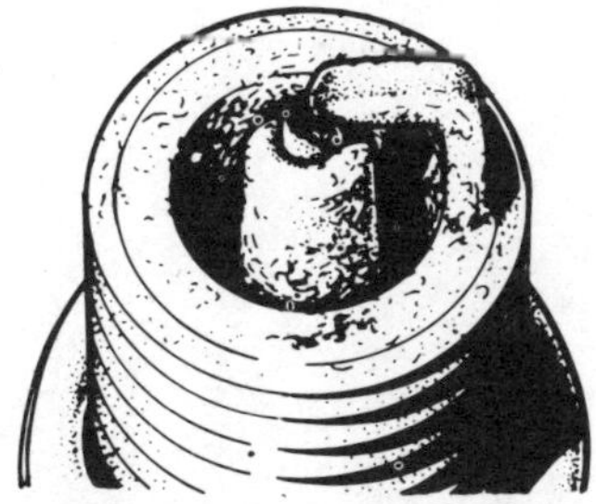

Mild white deposits and electrode burnt indicating too weak a fuel mixture

Plug in sound condition with light greyish brown deposits

Spark plug electrode conditions

now clearly visible and accessible. It will be seen that one point's located on a leaf spring which is moved by the four-lobe cam on the control spindle. To open the points, select top gear and with the handbrake released, rock the car to rotate the engine and enable the cam lobe to open the point to its fullest extent. (Alternatively, fit a spanner on the nut in the centre of the crankshaft pulley and turn the engine over in neutral).

The condition of the points is critical to their performance. If one has a high spot and the other a corresponding recess it's impossible to set the points gap accurately, and so they must be cleansed before adjusting, or if they're really in poor shape, renewed. The small high spot can be removed by carefully filing away or with fine emery, but this will mean removing the points and will take time and patience; care must be taken too to ensure that the point surfaces are kept parallel to each other. Any oil or grease which may be on the points should be washed off with petrol.

To set the gap between the contact points, open the points to the fullest extent by rotating the spindle cam (as described earlier), then insert the correct feeler gauge blade between the points. The blade must be a nice sliding fit – not tight and not loose. The correct gap requirement is 0.020 in (0.5 mm). Should the gap require adjustment, loosen the fixed contact point bracket retaining screw, then using a screwdriver pivot the contact bracket towards or away from the corresponding point as required to give the correct adjustment. Retighten the retaining screw, then recheck the gap.

Before replacing the rotor arm, lubricate the distributor where illustrated, with clean engine oil. The points indicated are (1) the felt pad – a few drops, (2) the reservoir hole – a teaspoonful and (3) the contact breaker cams – a smear of medium grease.

When replacing the rotor arm note that the lug in the rotor recess engages with the slot in the spindle. Before refitting the distributor cap, wipe it clean inside and out and examine it carefully for signs of hairline cracks. The carbon brush must be in good condition and held firmly by the spring which in turn is held by the cap. The four HT lead connections must be good and the four segments in the cap can be lightly cleaned by scraping with a penknife. If in doubt regarding the condition of the cap, change it for a new one but transfer each plug lead in turn so that you don't get confused over their respective locations.

9 Check valve clearances

The manufacturers recommend that the valve clearances are checked and set with the engine running but unless you're familiar with this method (in which case you probably won't need to read this!), we

Adjusting distributor points

Interior of distributor cap showing four contacts and central carbon brush

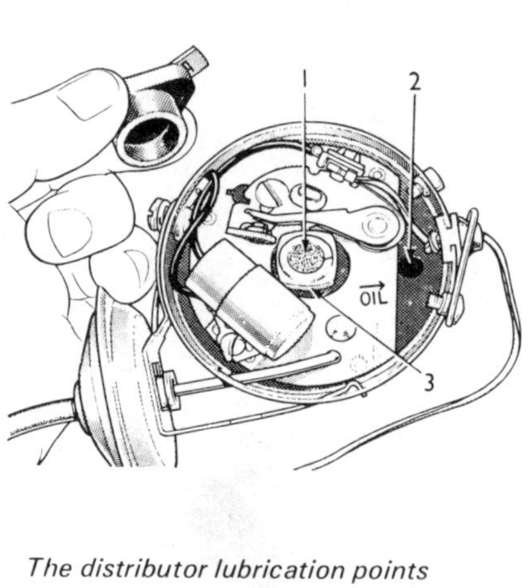

The distributor lubrication points

suggest you check them with the engine stopped. It should however be thoroughly warmed up to normal operating temperature (5 to 10 minutes from cold). It's a good idea to have a new rocker cover gasket available.

Take off the air cleaner for easier access and remove the wires and hose which are clipped to the rocker cover. Then undo the four securing screws and carefully lift off the cover and gasket. If the gasket's broken or hard and brittle it's best to replace it with a new one.

Valve clearances are checked between the end of the valve stem and the rocker arm, and this gap occurs when the valve is fully closed. The engine will need turning over and this is best done with a spanner fitted on the nut in the centre of the crankshaft pulley – the one at the bottom driving the fan belt. There are eight valves and for this procedure they 're numbered from 1 to 8 starting at the front of the engine. Not all have the same clearance.

Each valve's fully closed when a corresponding one is fully open (ie. when the rocker presses it fully down against the spring) and the table following shows this relationship. If the order's followed as shown the sequence will avoid unnecessary turning of the engine which can be tedious. This order can be

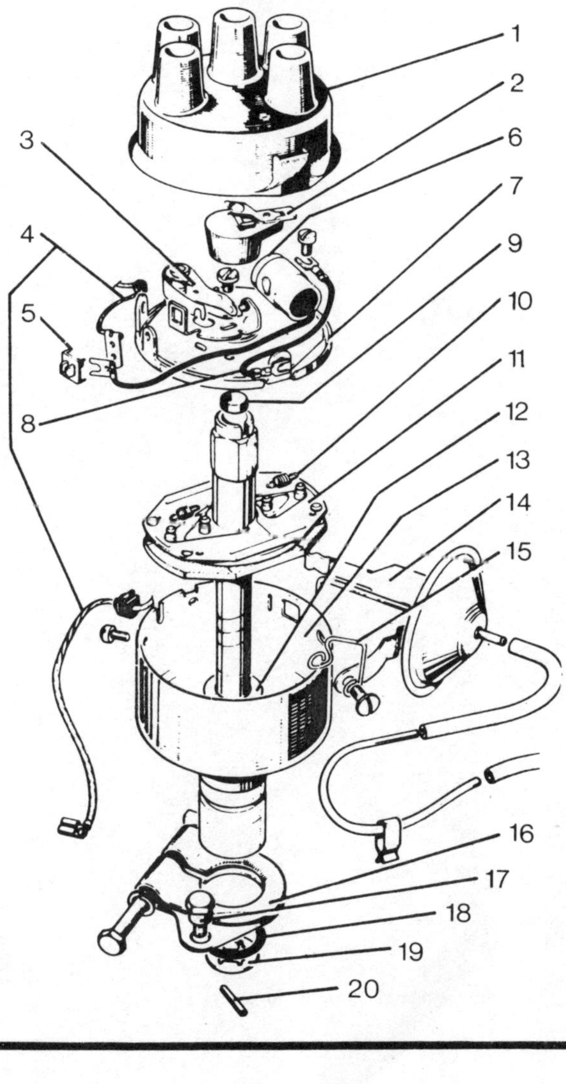

Ignition distributor component parts

1 Distributor cap
2 Rotor arm
3 Contact breaker assembly
4 Primary lead
5 Terminal insulator
6 Capacitor
7 Contact breaker
8 Earth lead
9 Felt pad
10 Centrifugal advance spring
11 Mainshaft and plate assembly
12 Upper thrust washer
13 Distributor body
14 Vacuum unit
15 Cap clip
16 Clamp plate
17 Bolt
18 Oil seal ring
19 Lower thrust washer
20 Pin

remembered if it's noted that each pair of valve numbers always adds up to 9. The correct clearance for each valve is shown. A feeler blade of the correct thickness should be inserted in each gap in turn accordingly. The gap's correct when a slight drag's felt on the blade as it's pulled through. To adjust the gap involves rotating the nut in the centre of the rocker arm and for this a tubular spanner must be used which doesn't foul the rocker arm when it's fitted over the nut. If the gap's too small to insert the feeler blade, turn the nut anticlockwise until the blade goes in and the gap's set. To close the gap turn the nut clockwise.

Valve being checked	*Clearance* (except '90' engines)*	*Corresponding valve*
No 1	0.010 inch (0.25 mm)	No 8
No 3	0.006 inch (0.15 mm)	No 6
No 5	0.010 inch (0.25 mm)	No 4
No 2	0.006 inch (0.15 mm)	No 7
No 8	0.010 inch (0.25 mm)	No 1
No 6	0.006 inch (0.15 mm)	No 3
No 4	0.010 inch (0.25 mm)	No 5
No 7	0.006 inch (0.15 mm)	No 2

*Note: On '90' engines all valve clearances are 0.008 inch (0.20 mm).

10 Check fan belt

It's most important that the fan belt is in good condition and correctly adjusted since it drives three components – the generator, the water pump and of course the cooling fan. If the belt's too tight, a greater strain is imposed on the generator and water pump bearings, shortening their working lives. If the belt's too loose it will slip, causing overheating and eventually a flat battery as well.

Adjustment is made by pivoting the generator to adjust the tension of the belt.

To check the tension, apply thumb pressure mid-way between the fan and generator pulleys; the depression should be about $\frac{1}{4}$ in (6 mm). To alter the tension, loosen the generator pivot mounting bolts and swing it outwards to increase the tension (using careful leverage if necessary) or inwards to decrease

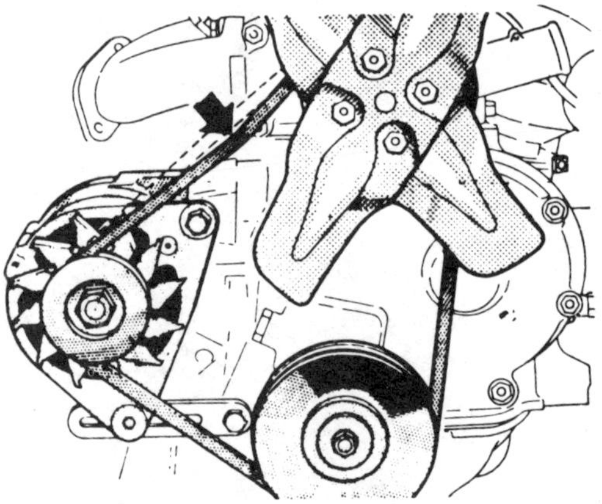

Fan belt adjustment

View of alternator (HC Viva) from below

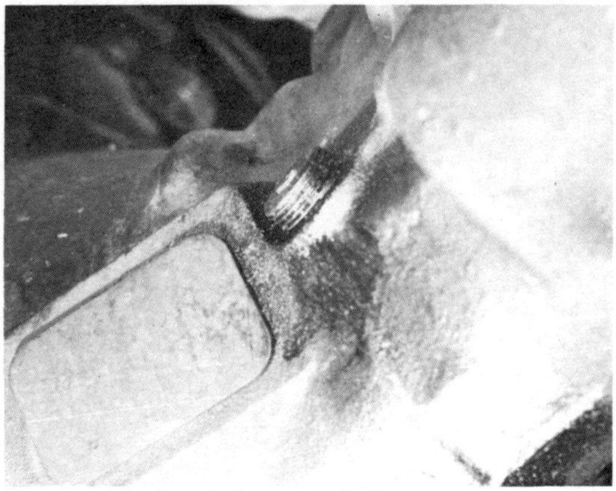

Gearbox filler/level plug (Viva HC)

it. Provided the bolts haven't been loosened too much, the generator should retain its position when they're retightened.

Check the belt for any signs of cracking or fraying and if it looks at all suspect, renew it. When a new fan belt's been fitted, recheck the tension after a nominal mileage as the belt may initially stretch.

11 Check gearbox oil level

On the left-hand side of the gearbox a square headed plug can be found which is the combined level and filler plug. Unless you've a pit or ramp it's difficult to check the level exactly because to get at the plug the car has to be jacked up and then it won't be level! However, place the car on level ground, jack it up on the left hand side, get underneath and thoroughly clean the area round the filler plug before removing it. Place a suitable container underneath to catch any overflow. There's little point in fiddling about trying to see where the level is, so add Castrol Hypoy 90 gear oil from one of the dispensers with a convenient flexible filler pipe, until the oil overflows and then let the car down off the jack, As you jacked up on the left side the gearbox will be slightly overfull so wait now until all overflow stops. Then jack the car up again and replace the filler/level plug firmly. Don't overfill the gearbox, as too much oil will cause pressure build-up, forcing oil out into the clutch housing or through the rear oil seal, which does no good at all.

Whatever you do, make sure you use the grade and type of oil specified – there's no drain plug, so you don't get a second chance!

Rear axle filler/level plug (Viva HC)

Zenith 3012 carburettor

1 Volume control screw
2 Throttle stop screw

12 Check rear axle oil level

The combined rear axle level and filler plug is located in the centre of the axle on the differential housing cover. There's no need to jack up the car as accessibility is good, but the car must be standing level. Before removing the plug, clean it and the surrounding area of the differential housing, and place the overflow container in position.

Again using Castrol Hypoy 90 from their convenient flexible dispensers, add oil until it overflows from the hole. Leave it a few minutes until the overflow stops and then replace the plug. Don't overfill with oil as it will only come out through the vent plug on the right-hand (top)of the axle casing. It's worthwhile checking that this vent plug's clear - otherwise pressure can build up and blow out the oil seals.

13 Check carburettor slow running adjustment

Solex/Zenith (fixed choke) type: If the engine idles unevenly or keeps stopping on tick-over it may be due to a small maladjustment on the carburettor. First get the engine completely warmed up. Then screw in the throttle stop screw on the carburettor so that the engine runs quickly enough to avoid stalling. Then turn the mixture control screw anticlockwise until the engine 'hunts' – that is, speeds up in intermittent but regular bursts. Then turn the same screw clockwise unitl the engine runs evenly. It will now be running too fast, so the throttle stop screw should be turned anticlockwise to reduce the engine speed. If, when the engine speed drops, the 'hunting' resumes, screw the mixture control in a little further.

Don't try and get the tick-over too slow – better a little too fast if anything. The Viva engine is high revving by design and is fussy at low tickover speeds.

Stromberg (variable choke) type: On '90' engines the principle of adjustment is the same but the jet adjuster (in place of the mixture control screw) is mounted in the base of the carburettor and if it's altered it means that the performance of the carburettor is altered at all engine speeds – not just tickover. The basic setting of the jet adjusting screw is three turns open. To check this it's necessary to remove the air cleaner complete with elbow. Then put a finger in the air intake to hold down the piston and screw in the jet adjusting screw until it touches the bottom of the piston. Then undo it three complete turns. Replace the air cleaner, run the engine until warm and then set the throttle stop screw to a fast idle speed. Adjust the jet mixture screw until the engine runs evenly. Any adjustment shouldn't exceed a $\frac{1}{2}$ turn in either direction. If uneven running's still apparent it must be caused by something else.

Readjust the throttle stop screw to give a reasonable tickover speed.

14 Check clutch pedal free play

Wear in the clutch won't be indicated by any significant change in the operation of the pedal but if the cable's not checked and adjusted the thrust release bearing could be subjected to unnecessary wear.

To adjust the cable, jack up the car and locate the end of the cable where it fits into the clutch operating lever. Unhook the return spring from the lever and move the lever in the opposite direction of the return spring action,. and at the same time pull the end of the cable in the other direction. There should be $\frac{1}{4}$ inch gap between the two. To increase the gap, undo the locknut and rotate the ball-ended adjuster as required. Tighten the locknut and reconnect the return spring after the adjustment's been made.

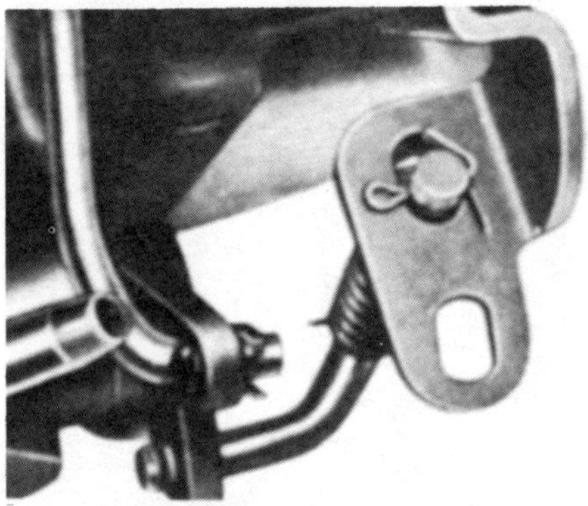

Zenith 12 Carburettor:– the accelerator pump rod setting holes for winter (shown) and summer

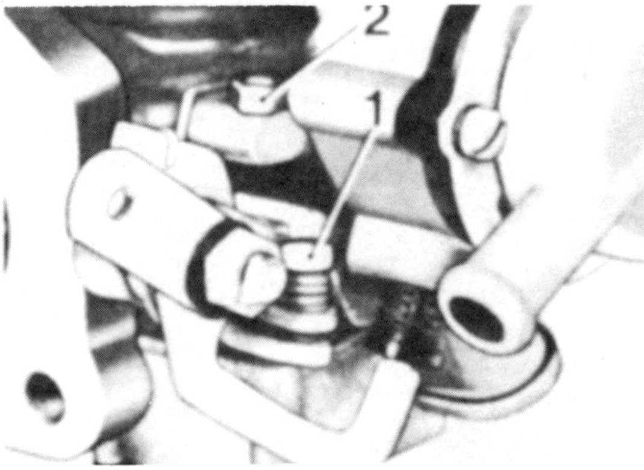

Stromberg 150 CDS carburettor

1 Throttle stop screw
2 Fast idle stop screw (adjust only when cold start device is dismantled)

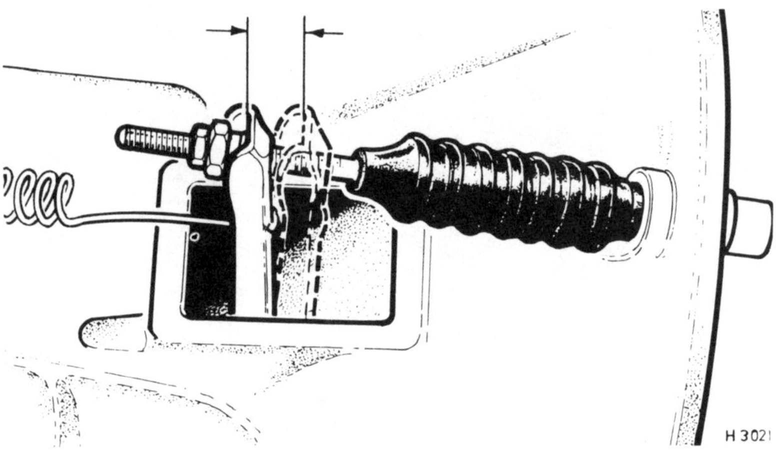

Clutch adjustment

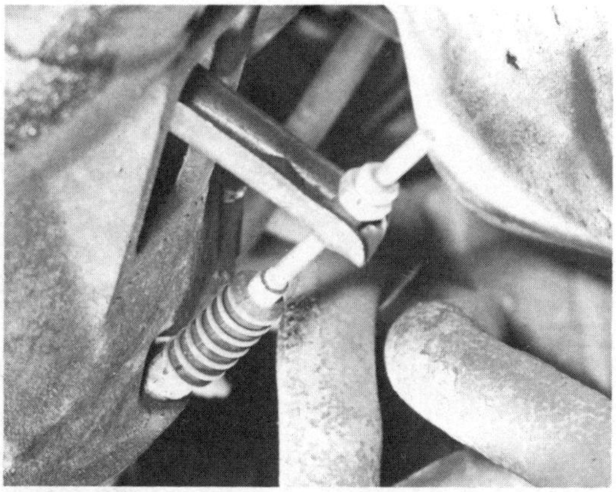

Clutch adjustment rod

View of nearside rear brake with drum removed (HC)

Withdrawal of pad retaining pin from front disc brake (Lockheed)

15 Check brake linings

Drum brakes: To examine drum brake linings, first jack up and support the car with chassis stands or blocks for additional support. Remove the roadwheel(s) and then the brake drum, which is attached to the hub by two hexagonal bolts. The brake adjusters will probably have to beslackened off two or three clicks to allow the drum to be withdrawn. If it won't pull off by hand, tap it lightly with a soft head hammer or mallet.

Having removed the drum, brush clean the linings and also inside of the drum. Both the linings and contact surfaces of the drum must be smooth and show no traces of oil. The linings are held in place on the shoes by rivets, the head of which must be at least 0.025 in (0.64 mm) below the surface of the lining. If the clearance is less than this figure on the linings are soaked in oil or brake fluid, they must be renewed and in the latter case the source of the leak found and rectified before using the car again. If the rivets are level with the lining surface and have scored the contact surface of the brake drum, both the linings and drum must be renewed.

Disc brakes: The disc brake pad thickness can be visually checked by jacking up the car at the front and removing each front wheel. The pads can now be seen between the disc and caliper body. Brush away any accumulated dust and road dirt and check that the pad friction material's at least 0.06 in (1.5 mm) thick. If they're under this thickness, they must be renewed. Replace both pads even if only one appears to be in need of renewing.

Renewing the pads isn't a particularly difficult job so why not have a go at it yourself? Start by removing the hydraulic fluid reservoir cap and syphon a small amount of fluid out to leave it about $\frac{1}{4}$ inch below the normal level mark. This is done to prevent any fluid overflowing when the level rises owing to the pistons being pressed in as described below. It's not essential provided you keep an eye on the reservoir level during this operation.

Remove the pads by withdrawing the clips from the retaining pins and extracting the pins. On Lockheed brakes the pins are split and spread to secure them, and there are also retaining spring plates behind them.Press the old pads against the pistons with the fingers to push the pistons back into the caliper, then lift out the pads and shims from the caliper body.

Insert the new pads (if the pistons still aren't pressed back sufficiently, lever them in carefully with a piece of hard wood or similar which won't damage them) and the shims, which should also be renewed if they're distorted or damaged.On Girling brakes, ensure that the shims are fitted with the arrow-shaped hole in the top edge pointing to the forward

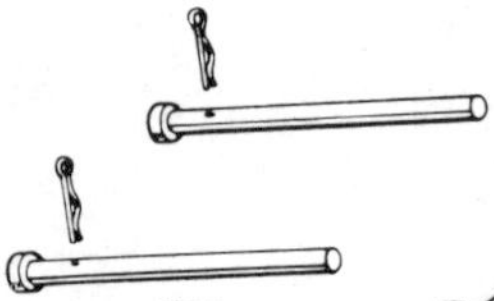

The Girling disc brake caliper components

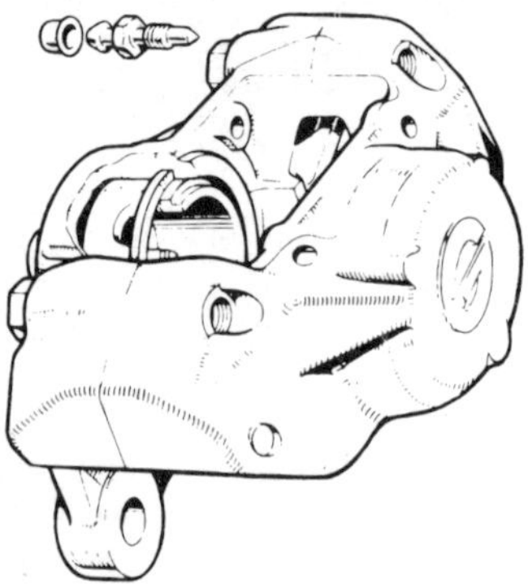

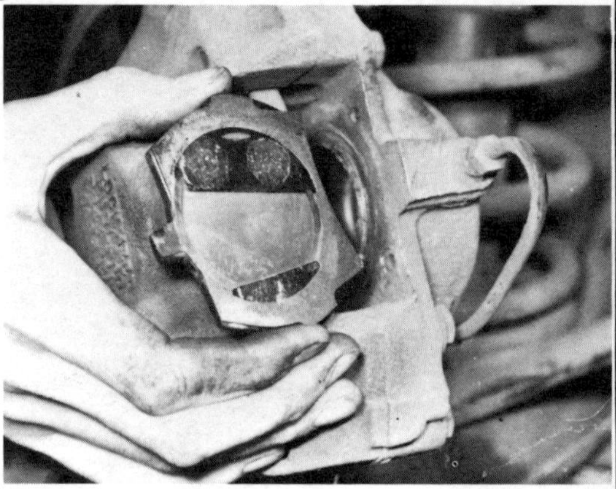

Pad and backing shim removed from caliper (Lockheed)

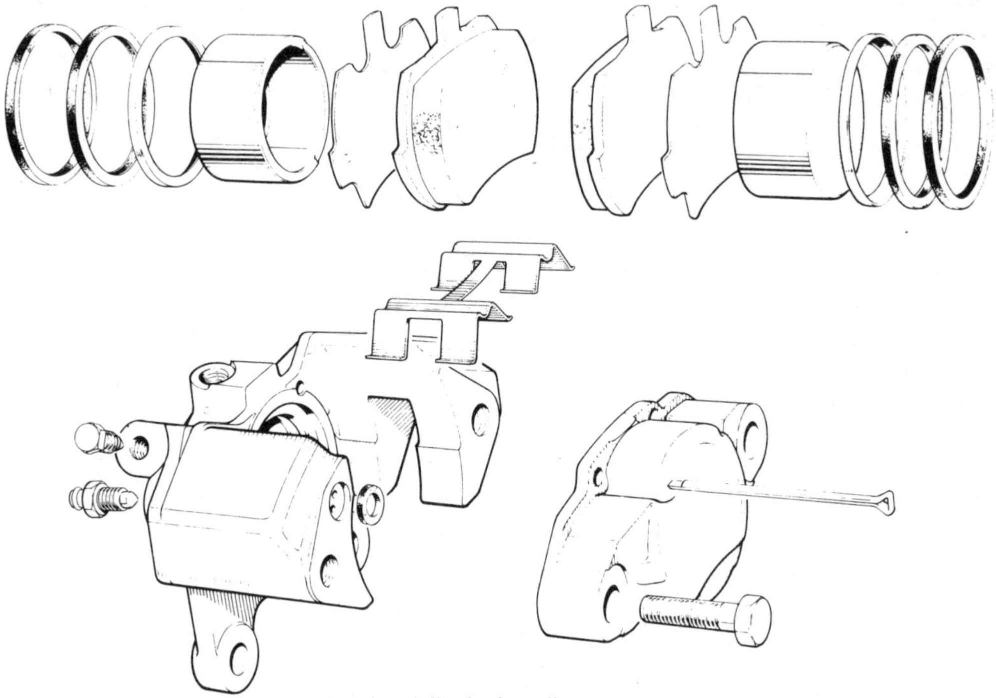

The Lockheed disc brake caliper components

disc rotation . (On Lockheed brakes the shims are symmetrical and it doesn't matter).

Refit the locating pins and clips. Now press the brake pedal two or three times to centralise the pistons, and top up the reservoir if necessary using new fluid, to the specified level. Remember that new pads will take a while to 'bed-in' and reach their full stopping power!

16 Renew brake servo air filter

On top of the brake servo unit there's a plastic cylindrical housing secured in position by a wire hoop clip. When the cover's lifted, the element can be removed. The old element can't be cleaned and therefore a new one has to be fitted. Wipe the interior of the cover and base clean before fitting the replacement element.

17 General checks

Check the engine, gearbox and rear axle for signs of excessive oil leaks and, if any are found, rectify or have the offending leak sealed as soon as possible.

Check the cooling system and hoses for signs of leakage or deterioration. Replace any hoses that look tired or perished.

Using engine oil, lubricate the throttle and clutch linkages and also the handbrake clevis joints. At the rear of the generator there is a cavity in the centre of the shaft bearing. Apply a few drops of Castrol Everyman or GTX into the hole to lubricate the porous bush.

Examine the full length of the seat belts particularly at loops and buckles where fraying may occur. See that the bolts at the anchorage points are tight, and get your garage to replace any suspect parts of the seat belts and mounting points.

EVERY 12 MONTHS OR 12,000 MILES

(in addition to those items covered in the 3,000 miles and 6,000 miles Service Schedule)

1 Renew carburettor air cleaner (paper element type)

Remove the element as described in the 6,000 mile Schedule. Discard the old element and replace with a new one, ensuring that the rubber sealing rings are correctly positioned round the raised centre sections in the cover and base.

2 Lubricate front suspension ball joints

Each of the steering joints, two at each side, has a grease nipple so that lubrication can be carried out. Access to them is easier if the wheel's removed, unless a pit or ramp is available. The joints should first be cleaned off and the rubber gaiters examined to make sure they're intact.

A few shots of grease with a molybdenum disulphide additive (Castrol MS3) from a grease gun are all that is needed. Do not over-lubricate in order to see grease ooze out. It will only ooze out when the rubber gaiters have either burst or aren't fitting correctly! If the gaiters are in poor condition, have them attended to at a garage together with the joints themselves.

3 Automatic transmission

Clean the ventilation holes and slots around the torque converter cover, and scrape clean the accumulation of dirt from the surrounding fittings.

4 Renew spark plugs

Remove and renew the spark plugs. Check the electrode gaps on the new ones as they may want

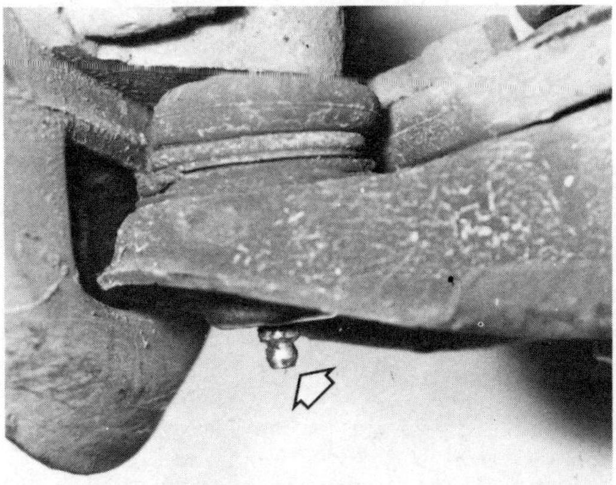

Front suspension upper and lower greasing nipples (arrowed)

resetting. If the old plugs still look serviceable, you can keep them as spares for an emergency should one of the new set let you down at any time.

5 Interchange roadwheels (if desired)

To ensure that the tyres wear evenly all round, they can be interchanged as shown in the illustration. Inspect the tyres for signs of uneven wear, cuts or defects and of course check that the tread depth meets the regulation specified. After retightening all the wheelnuts, check the tyre pressures. If your Viva's fitted with radial tyres, it's not generally recommended that these be changed around as it can upset the handling of the car.

6 General lubrication

Lightly lubricate the boot, bonnet and door hinges, catches and strikes with engine oil. Wipe off any surplus straight away – not on your best clothes later on!

EVERY 24 MONTHS OR 24,000 MILES

In view of the size and importance of this service which occurs only once every 24 months it is recommended that a complete professional check be carried out by an authorised Vauxhall dealer. Their experience will enable them to pinpoint certain defects or modifications which may not be covered in the normal scope of routine maintenance.

The two main items not covered in the foregoing work which occur on this Service are overhaul of the hydraulic braking system and removal and repacking with grease of the front wheel hub bearings.

Both these jobs call for more detailed dismantling and checking which is not within the scope of this Handbook. Alternatively the Haynes Owners Workshop Manual for your particular model of the Viva will give full details for this work.

Seasonal servicing

If you carry out the procedures we've detailed so far, at more or less the prescribed intervals of mileage or time, then you'll have gone a long way towards getting the best out of your Viva in terms of both performance and long life. That's the good news. The other kind is that there are always other areas, not dealt with in regular servicing schedules, where neglect can spell trouble.

We reckon a bit of extra time spent on your car at the beginning and end of the winter will be well repaid in terms of peace of mind and prevention of trouble. The suggested attentions which follow have therefore been divided into Spring and Autumn sections – but there's nothing to prevent you doing them more frequently if you like!

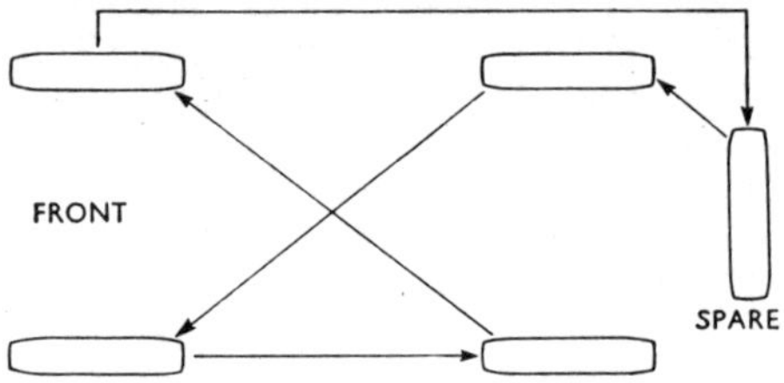

Suggested system of tyre rotation

Spring

We've put this one first as it's less depressing than Autumn – though there's probably more work involved...

Underside of Car

In Spring, we venture to suggest, the owner's fancy lightly turns to thoughts of cleaning off all the accumulated muck of winter from underneath the car. Without a shadow of doubt, the best time to clean underneath is the worst time from the discomfort point of view – that is, when the car's been driven in the wet and all the dirt's nicely softened up. So let's talk first about the easiest way out – steam cleaning or pressure washing. These aren't D-I-Y jobs, and can only be done at larger garages, usually those which undertake body repair jobs. You may feel this method's unnecessarily expensive, but it's generally preferable to grovelling about underneath and getting filthy and uncomfortable doing it yourself. However, for the owner who really wants to do it by hand, here goes...

You'll need paraffin or a water-soluble solvent, water (and preferably a hose), a wire brush, a scraper and a stiff-bristle brush. If you think the car floor may leak, remove the carpets or they'll get wet; this will also help you pinpoint the places where water's getting in.

To start with, jack the car up as high as possible, preferably at one side or one end. For your own safety, support it on ramps or concrete or wooden blocks and chock the wheels which are on the ground. Unless both rear wheels are raised, also apply the handbrake and engage first or reverse gear.

Now get underneath (you've put it off as long as you can!) and cover the brake discs and calipers (where applicable) with polythene bags to stop mud and water getting into them. Next loosen any encrusted dirt and, working from one end or one side, scrape or brush it away. The paraffin or solvent can be used where there's oil contamination. After all the brushing and scraping, a final wash down with the hose will remove the last of the dirt and mud.

You can now check for leaks in the floor; if you find any, dry the area carefully then use a mastic type sealer to plug the offending gap. Hollow sections of doors and bodywork can be sprayed or brush-painted with a rust-inhibitor to provide some extra protection. If there are signs of the underseal breaking away, this is a good opportunity to patch it up. Undersealing paint is available in spray cans or tins from accessory shops; one small point about putting the stuff on though, and that's to make sure the area is clean and dry, otherwise you're wasting your time.

While you're underneath, have a good look round for signs of rusting. Likely places are the body sills, floor panels and bodywork around the wheels generally; if you do find any rust have a word with the local Vauxhall man or body repair shop before things get too bad. Check too that the drain holes in body sills and doors are clear – if necessary poke out any obstruction with a piece of thin wood.

Bodywork

This too will have suffered from all the muck and salt that's around during the winter, and there's no better time to wash it thoroughly and check for stone chips and rust spots. Your're bound to find some despite the regular washing you've given the car – or meant to – throughout the winter. Treat as for rusty scratches (see *Body Beautiful*).

After the touch-up paint has thoroughly hardened, it's worth giving the car a good polish to prepare it for the long, hot summer ahead (well, there's no harm in hoping). If you're feeling really energetic you could do the interior as well but the most important cleaning jobs are now done.

Engine air cleaner intake (where applicable)

Again in anticipation of warmer weather to come, the position of the carburettor air intake should be changed from the winter to summer setting. On some models the intake spout can be set so that it either draws in warm air from the exhaust manifold, or cooler air from the engine compartment generally. Positioning the intake to draw in warmer air during winter obviously makes sense because it helps to warm the ingoing mixture and enables the choke to be used less. But now the outside temperature should be warm enough and the summer position is the correct one.

Remember to tighten the nut or screw after adjusting.

Autumn

With winter on the way, your car's electrical system is going to take much more of a beating than it has during the last few months. Now – and not on a dark night miles from anywhere in a snowstorm – is the time to check the vital components. Where other Sections or Chapters are referred to in brackets, the detailed procedure's described there.

Drain holes in body sill

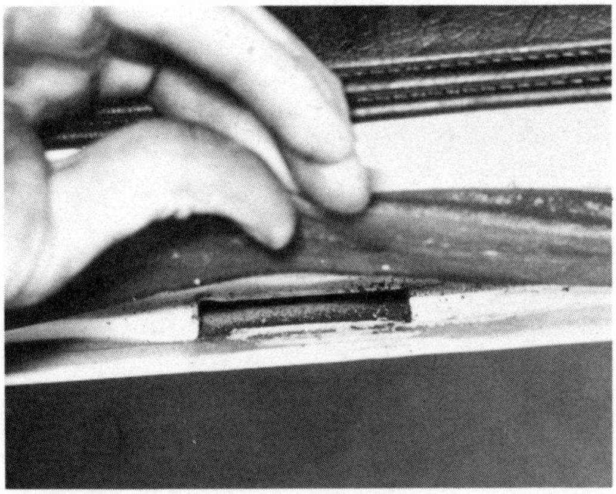

Drain holes in door

Battery

Ensure this is topped up correctly *(Weekly Section).*

Check and clean as necessary *(3000 miles)*

Fan belt

Check and adjust *(6000 miles)*

Lights

Check operation *(3000 miles)*

Renew any failed bulbs *(In an Emergency)* or check for faults as necessary *(Troubleshooter 6).*

Wipers/Washers

These are going to get a lot of use, so check the

wiper arms and blades *(3000 miles).* Top up washer reservoir *(Weekly Section)* and check operation.

Carburettor Air Intake

Reset to winter position *(Spring Section).*

Cooling system

Check all hoses *(6000 miles).*

Check that the antifreeze solution in the engine cooling system's of the correct strength or, if there's no antifreeze in, add some as described below. 'Bluecol' antifreeze or equivalent is recommended and can be left in the cooling system for up to two years. If you have antifreeze in already but are uncertain of its strength, it's advisable to have the specific gravity of the coolant checked by your garage.

The recommended solutions (by volume) and quantities for the Viva are as follows:

%	*Quantity*	*Complete protection down to*
25	$2\frac{1}{2}$ pints (1·4 litres)	−11°C (12°F)
35	$3\frac{1}{2}$ pints (1·9 litres)	−19°C (−2°F)
45	$4\frac{1}{2}$ pints (2·5 litres)	−29°C (−20°F)

A 25% solution should give adequate protection in most parts of Britain, but to be on the safe side the 35% mixture is preferable.

Radiator antifreeze mustn't be used in the screenwash system as it's harmful to paintwork. Special additives can be obtained for the screenwash reservoir to prevent freezing up during winter.

Useful aerosols

When next at your local garage or accessory shop it's a good idea to get a can of 'Damp-Start' or similar ignition waterproofer, and you'll probably need a can of windscreen de-icer at your disposal sometime during the coming winter months. These items should be carried in the car so that they're always on hand when needed in damp or icy conditions.

Body Beautiful

A car always seems to go that much better when it's clean – whether this is true or purely psychological is open to argument. What can't be denied is that a car with clean, glossy paintwork and tidy interior generally gives the owner more satisfaction and pride of ownership than one that's allowed to deteriorate both in looks and value. If a car's in good all round condition when you buy it, then there isn't too much effort involved in keeping it that way. But if your Viva was obviously neglected by its previous owner(s) then a little extra effort's required to restore some of the former 'glory' – provided it isn't too far gone when you start!

Some people regard car cleaning as one of the joyful aspects of ownership, others look on it as a tedious task and a necessary evil. If you fall into the latter category, then the best plan of action is to do a little each week, dividing the job into sections. In this way you'll at least maintain a reasonable standard of appearance and break up the monotony of the job.

The really keen types won't only have the interior and bodywork dazzling, but will also keep the engine free of oil and dirt. Though you may be horrified at the idea, it's not a bad one when you think about it. For one thing, if you do carry out any repairs on the engine or surrounding components, the job will be made that much easier and more pleasant just because you'll keep yourself cleaner and be able to see what you're doing. Another point is that any oil or water leaks can easily be traced at an early stage and rectified before they get really serious.

If you only recently got your Viva and the engine's barely visible through the coating of muck, the easiest way to clean it, as with the underside, is to take it along to a garage equipped with a steam cleaner. For a small cash outlay, this will save you a lot of time and effort, and thereafter the engine can be occasionally wiped clean using a rag lightly dampened in paraffin. If you decide to clean it by hand, scrape off the worst of the dirt, then brush on a solvent such as Gunk or Jizer and hose off the remainder, but remember to seal your ignition leads, distributor and coil or that nice clean engine will prove difficult to start again!

If you've bought this book intending to do all the routine servicing of your car yourself, then you'll surely want to keep the bodywork and inside of the car looking good too. And for anyone who doesn't, here's how to do it anyway ...

It's always a good idea to clean the interior first; this way you won't get the dust all over your nicely polished exterior – or the car's! Begin by removing all the contents, not forgetting the odds and ends in the pockets and glovebox. Then take out all the mats and carpets, which should be shaken and brushed, or better still vacuum-cleaned. If they need further cleaning this can be done with a carpet shampoo, but let them dry thoroughly before you put them back. Any underfelt should be taken out and shaken, too, but don't try washing this or it may end up in rather more pieces than you started with.

If the carpets should just happen to be in such a bad state of decay that they don't merit cleaning, why not get yourself a decent set of replacements... You can get kits tailored for your particular model from specialist firms, and they're quite reasonably priced.

The inside of the car can now be cleaned with a brush and dustpan, or again preferably, a vacuum cleaner. If the flex on the Hoover won't stretch to the car (and the car won't squeeze through the front door!) it might be worth thinking about investing in one of the small 12-volt hand vacuums which can be attached to your car battery – your accessory shop can probably show you one.

Seat and trim materials can be wiped over with warm water containing a little washing-up liquid, but for best results (particularly if they're very dirty) use one of the proprietary upholstery cleaners such as Decosol, which are specially made for the job. An old nail brush will help to remove ingrained marks, but don't splash too much water about and do wipe the surfaces dry afterwards with a clean cloth, leaving the windows open to speed up drying. The carpets can be put back when they're quite dry, making sure they're properly fitted around the controls etc.

You have to be careful about cleaning car windows, especially the windscreen, with some household products as these can leave a smeary film. Water containing a few drops of ammonia is probably best, but any stubborn marks and smears can be removed with methylated spirit; finish off with a chamois leather squeezed as dry as possible.

Just in case you should think that's it, there's still the boot to be dealt with. Take out that collection of junk that seems to have grown every time you open the lid, and get busy with brush or vacuum cleaner again. While you're at it, if you must carry all that stuff around, now's the time to try and stow it so it doesn't rattle any more!

Now you can pause for a moment – make a well-earned cup of tea perhaps – and take a critical look at the interior. Are there any nicks or tears in the seats or other trim? Is the headlining drooping or peeling? Some excellent products can now be obtained for repairs such as these. One of the most useful is probably the vinyl repair kit, which comes in various colours and consists of a quantity of 'liquid vinyl' and some sheets of texturing material. The liquid's applied to a split or hole in a plastic seat or piece of trim, smoothed like body filler, and allowed to set. It's then blended into the surrounding area by selecting the best matching pattern from the graining material supplied, placing this over the repair and rubbing with a hot iron; the pattern's then embossed into the repaired area. This type of repair's equally successful, incidentally, on vinyl roofs if your car happens to have one.

For larger splits or tears it may be necessary to cut a piece of matching material from somewhere that doesn't show, apply some suitable adhesive to it and work it under the edges of the tear, pressing these together as neatly as possible once the glue has become tacky enough. Any loose headlining or trim can also be stuck in place – but make sure you get an adhesive that's suitable for PVC or vinyl.

Once you've got the seats in a reasonable state of cleanliness and repair, why not consider seat covers... Like the carpets, they're available from specialist firms to suit your car and are a worthwhile buy in view of the protection they give.

If you use your car regularly and you've got the time and inclination, it should really be washed every week, either by hand (preferably using a hosepipe) or by taking advantage of the local car-wash if there is one. Whichever method you choose (assuming you wash your car at all!) we don't think we need tell you how to do it – but remember it's never a good idea to just wipe over a very dirty car, whether wet or dry; you might as well sandpaper it!

Two or three times a year (even once is better than not at all) a good silicone or wax polish can be used on the paintwork. We don't know which of the many makes you'll use, so we can only recommend you to follow the makers' instructions closely so that you do see a reward for your efforts. Chrome parts are best cleaned with a special chrome cleaner; ordinary metal polish will attack the finish.

If the paint's beginning to lose its gloss or colour, and ordinary polishing doesn't seem to help, it will be worth considering the use of a polish with a mild 'cutting' action to remove what is, in effect, a surface layer of dead paint. Your friendly neighbourhood accessory shop man will advise on a suitable type.

The remainder of this Chapter describes how to keep your car's bodywork and paintwork in good condition by dealing with scratches and more major damage too, as they occur. A number of repair aids and materials are referred to, most of them essential if you're to achieve good results. They should all be available, together with free advice, from good motor accessory shops.

Keeping paintwork up to scratch

With superficial scratches (the sort only other people seem to get) where they don't penetrate down to the metal, you'll be glad to hear that repair can be very simple. Lightly rub the area with a paintwork renovator or a fine cutting paste to remove any loose paint from the scratch and to clean off any polish. Rinse the area with plenty of clean water and allow to dry. Apply touch-up paint to the scratch using a fine brush, and continue to build up the paint by several applications, allowing each to dry, until it's level with the surrounding area. Allow the new paint at least two weeks to harden (knitting or a crossword puzzle will help to pass the time) then use the paint renovator or cutting paste again to blend it into the original. Now a good polish can be used.

For anyone who's as lazy as we are, the easy alternative to painting over a scratch is to use a 'paint transfer', available in packs to match popular car colours. Prepare the affected area in the same way as for touch-up paint, then simply pick a transfer of a suitable size to cover the scratch completely. Hold the transfer against the area and burnish its backing paper, and if you're doing it right you should find it sticks to the car paintwork (rather than your hand) and at the same time frees itself from the backing. The patched area can now be polished to blend it in.

When you've got a scratch that's penetrated right through to the metal, causing rusting, you need a different technique. Use your Scout knife to remove any loose rust from the bottom of the scratch, then paint on a rust-inhibiting paint to prevent it from spreading. You'll probably now need to apply celulose body stopper paste – use a rubber or nylon applicator or a knife, but don't borrow one from the kitchen as

Arrows indicate points at which rust is likely to occur

you'll have a job cleaning it!

The paste can be thinned down if necessary using cellulose thinners. Before it happens, it's a good idea to wrap a piece of smooth cotton rag round the end of your finger, dip it in thinners and quickly sweep it across the filled scratch. This ensures that the area's very slightly hollowed and allows the paint to be built up to the correct level as described earlier.

Dealing with dents

When your car's bodywork gets a deep depression, you'll probably have one too. But there's no reason why even fairly large dents can't be tackled successfully by the D-I-Y owner, especially using the excellent body repair materials now available. So cheer up, and let's see what can be done.

The first step is to try to pull the dented metal out to bring it more or less back to the original level. Don't expect to make a perfect job of this – you won't; the metal has stretched and 'work-hardened' which makes it a virtually impossible job. Try to bring the level up to about $\frac{1}{8}$ inch below the surrounding area; obviously, with shallow dents you can bypass this bit. If the underside of the dent can be got at, try hammering it out gently from behind, using a hammer with a wooden or plastic head. You'll need to hold a fairly heavy hardwood block on the outside of the dent; this absorbs the impact of the hammer blows and helps to stop the metal being dented in the opposite direction!

If you've got a dent in a completely enclosed body section, or there's something else preventing you from getting behind it, a different approach is needed. Try to screw up enough courage to drill several small holes through the metal in the dent, particularly in the deeper parts. Now screw in several self-tapping screws so that they get a good bite, and either pull on the heads with pliers or wrap some heavy gauge steel wire round them and pull this. Brace yourself in case something gives suddenly or you may dent your own bodywork!

Now to remove the paint from the damaged area. This is best done using a power drill and abrasive disc, but if you've got the time and energy you can use elbow-grease and abrasive paper. Don't forget to remove the paint from an inch or so of the surrounding good paintwork, too, so that everything blends in nicely. New score the metal surface with a screwdriver or the tang of a file to provide a good key for the filler which you're going to have to apply, in case you didn't know. Now, to finish off the repair, refer to the filling and spraying section at the end of this Chapter.

Rust holes and gashes

If there's any paint left on the affected area, remove it as described previously so that you can get a good idea of just how bad the problem is. If there's more rust or fresh air than good metal, now's the time to consider whether a replacement panel would be more appropriate; this is a body shop job, beyond the scope of this book.

If things don't seem that bad and you're prepared to have a go at doing the job yourself, remove all the fittings from the surrounding area except those which may help to give a good guide to what the shape should be (eg, headlamp shells). Now, get a hacksaw blade or a pair of snips and cut out all the loose and badly affected metal. Hammer the edges inwards so that you've got a recessed area to build up on.

Wire brush the edges to remove any powdery rust, then paint over with a rust inhibitor; if you can get to the back, do the same to that. You're now going to fill the hole with something, but unfortunately just anything won't do. The best bets are zinc gauze, aluminium tape or polyurethane foam. The gauze is probably the favourite for a large hole. Cut a piece slightly larger than the hole to be filled, then position it in the hole so that its edges are below the level of the surrounding bodywork. If necessary, hold it in place with a few blobs of filler paste. For small or narrow holes you can use the aluminium tape which is sold by the roll. Pull off a piece of trim to the approximate size and shape required. If there's backing paper, peel it off (it sticks better that way) and place the tape over the hole; if necessary, pieces can be overlapped at the edges. Burnish down the edges of the tape with a file handle or similar to make sure it's firmly adhering to the metal.

Polyurethane foam is best used in hollow body sections, but if you're using this follow the makers' instructions carefully. When this foam hardens it can be cut back to just below the level of the surrounding bodywork with a hacksaw blade.

With the hole now blocked off, the affected area can be filled and sprayed as follows.

Filling and spraying

Many types of body filler are available, but generally speaking those proprietary kits which contain filler paste (or a filler powder and resin liquid) and a separate hardener are best. You'll also need a flexible plastic or nylon applicator (usually supplied) for putting the mixture on with. Mix up a little of the filler on a piece of board or plastic (those plastic margarine tubs are ideal but do wash out all traces of the contents first!). Read the instructions carefully and don't make up too much at one go. You'll find you have to work fairly fast or the mixture will begin to set, especially if you've been a bit generous with the hardener.

Apply the paste to the prepared hole or dent more or less to the correct level and contour, but don't try to shape it once it's become tacky or it'll pick up on the applicator. Layers should be built up at intervals until the final level's just proud of the surrounding bodywork.

When the filler's fully hardened, use a Surform plane or coarse file to remove the excess and obtain the final shape. Then follow with progressively finer grades of wet-or-dry abrasive paper starting with corase, followed by medium, then fine (some manufacturers give 'grit' grades to their wet-or-dry paper – 40 is the coarsest, 400 the finest). Always wrap the paper round a flat block if you're trying to get a flat surface, and keep it wet by rinsing in clean water, or the filler and paint will clog up the abrasive surface.

At this point, the doctored area should be surrounded by a ring of bare metal, encircled by a feathered edge of good paintwork. Rinse it with plenty of clean water to get rid of all the paint and filler dust, and allow it to dry completely.

If you're happy with the surface you've obtained then you're ready to apply some paint. First spray over the whole area with a light coat of grey primer. This will show up any surface imperfections which may need further treatment, and will also help you get the knack of spraying with an aerosol can before you start on the colour coats. Rub down the surface again, and if necessary use a little body stopper, as described for minor scratches, to fill any small imperfections. Repeat this spray-and-level procedure until you're satisfied with the finish; then wash down again and allow to dry.

The next stage is to apply the finishing coats, but first a word or two about the techniques involved. Paint spraying should be done in a warm, dry, windless, dust-free atmosphere – conditions not very readily available to most of us! You may be able to approach them artificially if you've got a large indoor workshop, but if you have to work outside you'll need to pick the day carefully. If you're working in your garage you'll probably need to 'lay' the dust on the floor by damping it with water.

If the body repair's confined to a small patch, mask off the surrounding area to protect it from paint spray. Bodywork fittings (chrome strips, door handles and the like) will need to be either masked or removed. If you're masking, use genuine masking tape and plenty of newspaper as necessary. Before starting to spray, shake the aerosol can thoroughly; then experiment on something (an old tin or similar will do – not the neighbours' car!) until you feel you can apply the paint smoothly. At the previous stage this wasn't too important, but now you're trying to get the best possible finish.

First cover the repair area with a thick coat of primer – not as one coat, but built up of several thin ones. When this is dry, using the finest wet-or-dry paper, rub down the surface until it's really smooth. Use plenty of water to keep the surface clean; when it's dry, spray on another primer coat and repeat the procedure.

Now for the top coat. Again the idea's to build up the paint thickness by several thin coats. Have a test spray first as this is a different aerosol, then commence spraying in the centre of the repair area. Using a circular motion, work gradually outwards towards the edges until the whole of the repair and about two inches of the surrounding original paint is covered. Remove all the masking material 10 to 15 minutes after you've finished spraying.

Now you can start putting away all the bits and pieces because it'll need about two weeks for the paint to harden completely. After this time, using a paint renovator or a very fine cutting paste, blend the edges of the new paint into the original. Finally, apply a good wax or silicone polish, and hopefully you'll have a repair you're proud to own up to!

Adding 'Pinstripes'

There are various kinds of self-adhesive body decor available for customising your car, while some models of the Viva have their own side-stripes built in. Perhaps the neatest and most suitable of the 'add-on' variety are Pinstripes, and we've included these in this Chapter as they may appeal to the owner who wants a cheap and simple way to improve the appearance of his or her car. They're adhesive tapes which come in different widths and colours and as single or multi-stripes. Most have a backing paper which is peeled off as the stripe is applied.

When applying any of these self-adhesive tapes, first make sure the paintwork's clean by washing with warm water and a car shampoo or liquid detergent. Next clean up the surface with a very fine cutting paste or paintwork renovator, and wash down again. You can now apply the tape, but follow the directions carefully. Smooth it down with a clean rag and, if necessary, prick out any small air bubbles with a pin. Try not to stretch the stripes as you put them on because they'll shrink slightly anyway; and wrap the ends round the panels so that they don't pull away at the edges.

The Personal Touch

A vast multitude of accessories are available these days to enable you to transform even the most basic Viva model into the 'luxury' class. Go into the average accessory shop and you're faced with such a line-up of 'special offers' that if you're not careful you'll be broke before you're halfway round this Aladdin's Cave of motoring paraphernalia, so first sort out your most immediate needs and give them priority.

Vauxhall Motors market a wide range of accessories that are tailor-made to fit your Viva model and of course you'll get expert fitting advice from your Vauxhall dealers. If the item you want isn't in the Vauxhall range, or a similar product's more competitively priced from a general accessory shop, make sure first that it's suitable for your model and secondly that you're able, and have the tools required, to install it. Many accessory packs today list the car models that they'll fit, but check with the supplier before buying.

All good products will be supplied with general fitting instructions which may or may not require minor modifications to suit your Viva. If you're buying secondhand, of course, you may get no instructions at all. The guidelines given here are in no way intended to replace the manufacturers' instructions, and if you're in doubt about fitting a particular item, they're the people to refer to.

We'd need several volumes to discuss all the various kinds of things you might conceivably buy for your car, and those we have managed to mention can't be gone into in great detail in a book like this. Some time spent browsing around a good motor accessory shop will reveal more than we can here, but nevertheless we hope the suggestions given may prove useful.

NOTE: always disconnect the battery before commencing any work involving the electrical system. Fireworks are very pretty, but there's a time and place for everything.

Auxiliary Instruments

It would be possible to write a complete book on auxiliary instruments and how to fit them but, as with other things, you'll normally get pretty good instructions when you buy them. Because there are so many instruments available, we're only going to consider ammeters, battery condition indicators, clocks, oil pressure gauges, tachometers, and vacuum gauges.

First of all, even before you've decided what instruments you're going to fit, you've got to think where to fit them. The dash panel of the Viva models doesn't lend itself readily to fitting brackets and small extra panels, because the instruments will end up being rather low down. Some instruments such as tachometers can be pod types, which are attached to the top of the dash panel. Another answer may be a central console, which will not only allow you to mount instruments but may have a radio installation compartment and/or a storage pocket. Some information on these is given later in this Chapter.

Sooner or later you're going to have to start drilling some holes somewhere, but this needn't cause any real headaches if it's approached in the right way. Make sure there's nothing behind the panel before even considering drilling a hole, and that there's enough room to fit the instrument, switch, or whatever, in the space chosen. Any hole which will have a cable or capillary running through it must have a plastic or rubber grommet to prevent the metal chafing through; these grommets can be obtain from D-I-Y accessory or car electrical shops.

Ammeter

The ammeter must be connected in such a way that it registers all the current supplied to, or drawn from, the battery except for the starting circuit. On models fitted with an alternator you'll need an instrument that reads to plus and minus 40 amperes, while for the earlier models fitted with a dynamo, an ammeter with a reading of plus and minus 30 amps is acceptable.

It's essential that the wiring's correct and that a heavy gauge of wire is used, so follow the fitting instructions carefully, or get expert advice before you

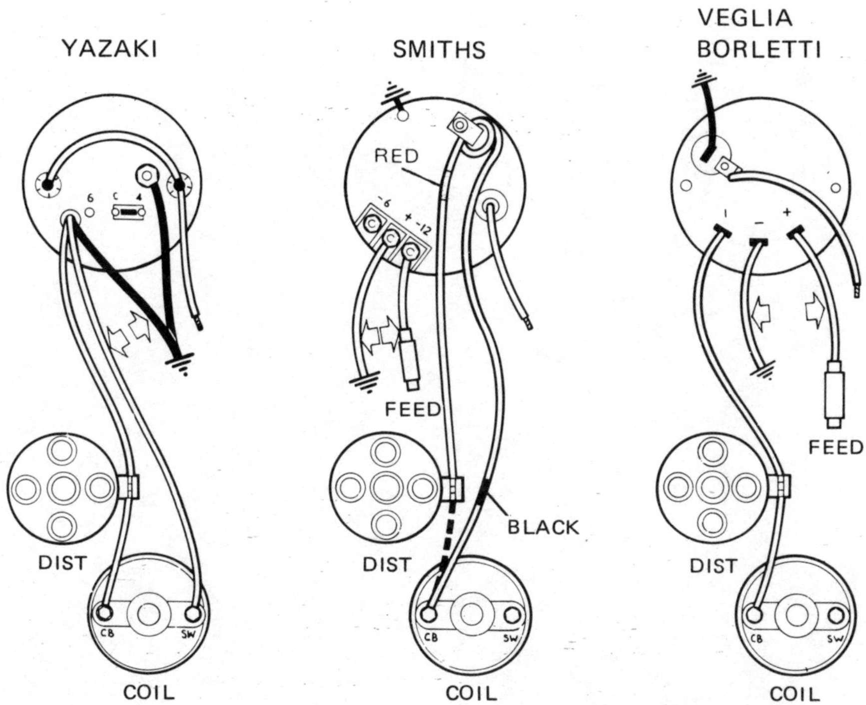

Connections for three popular tachometers

Yazaki:	*Negative earth shown – reverse arrowed wires to change polarity.*
Smiths:	*Positive earth shown – the dotted connection must be removed when the tachometer is fitted.*
	Reverse arrowed wires to change polarity.
Veglia Borletti:	*Negative earth shown – reverse wires to change polarity.*

start. If, after the ammeter's connected, it's found to be indicating in the reverse sense, simply change over the connections on the back of the instrument.

Battery condition indicator

The battery condition indicator's simply a voltmeter, and as such must be connected to a good earth point on the chassis and to any suitable connection which is live when the ignition switch is ON. For convenience, this could be the fuse for the direction indicator or windscreen wiper circuits. You won't need heavy cables for the battery condition indicator, 14/0·30 (14/·012) should be OK, but make sure that the earth polarity's correct.

Clock

Clocks come in many forms, but most types contain semi-conductors. If this means nothing to you, remember that while it ensures a negligible load on the battery it does mean that the polarity (positive/negative connections) is critical if you don't want to cause permanent damage, so watch the makers' instructions here. Connections are much the same as for the battery condition indicator except that you don't want the clock to stop when the ignition's switched off. Therefore a suitable connecting point should be the fuse for the interior light etc.

Tachometer

The tachometer (rev counter) is the one instrument that's available in larger sizes than the others (80 mm instead of 52 mm, although the smaller size can be obtained). Most are positive *or* negative earth, but you must connect them up correctly. In case you should pick up a secondhand one, connections for the most common types are shown in the illustrations. Note that with the Smiths type, the distributor-to-coil LT lead is removed; also note the sleeve colours on the main white lead. Use a 14/0·30 (14/·012) cable size.

Some of the supplementary instruments and other accessories available from Smiths Industries

Oil Pressure Gauge

If you really care about your engine then this is a must. The oil pressure warning light will only inform you that something is wrong when it's possibly too late or too inconvenient to do anything about it. The pressure gauge indicates the engine oil pressure, which in turn tells you the basic condition of your engine; any sudden or gradual decline in pressure can be noted and the fault rectified before the situation's serious. Two types of gauge are available – the mechanical type, with a small-bore copper or nylon tube to the gauge from the engine, and the electrical type in which an electrical sensing device transmits a varying voltage to the gauge. With both types a 'T' connection will be required to enable the existing oil pressure warning light to be retained as well.

Vacuum gauge (performance gauge or fuel consumption gauge)

This is simple a suction (negative pressure) meter which screws into the tapping on the inlet manifold, with a flexible pipe to the gauge. Once you've got the hang of using it, it can be very useful as an aid to economical driving – see Save It!

Consoles

These come in all shapes, sizes and prices. If your Viva's not already fitted with a console and you're thinking of buying one, have a good look round to see what's on the market - that includes looking through the motoring D-I-Y magazines. Some types extend back from the engine compartment wall or dash panel to behind the handbrake, the handbrake and gear levers coming up through the console base panel. You can get them with cut-outs for switches, radios and tape players, and for the standard 52 mm diameter circular instruments. Many types also have an ashtray or storage pocket, some also have an arm-rest; there's even a type that fits to the roof! They come in a variety of finishes, black leatherette, fibreglass, or woodgrain, and in various colours. Without a great deal of difficulty your should be able to get something that suits both your taste and your pocket.

Fitting's usually straightforward, but you may need to drill a few holes which could lead to your buying some self-tapping screws as well. Before drilling, don't forget to look what's on the other side of the panel, or your console could prove rather expensive.

Warning Devices

Air Horns

Air horns are marketed by several companies as a D-I-Y instillation kit comprising the horns themselves,

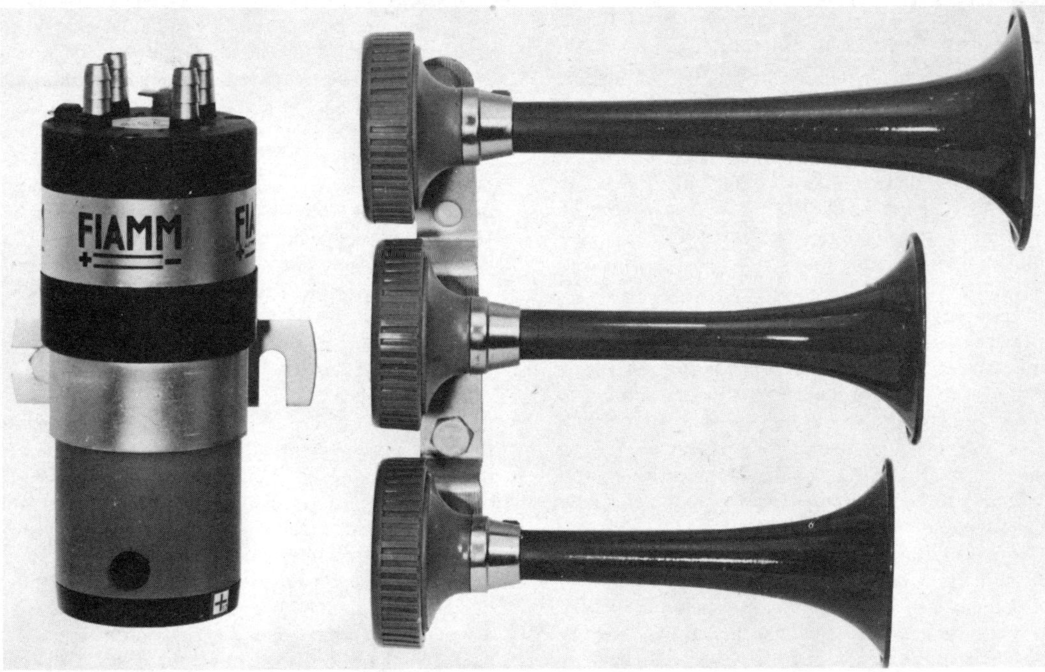

Fiamm 'Trio' air horns

a compressor unit, a relay, plastic piping and electrical cable. What you've obviously got to do is mount the horns reasonably near the compressor, and the compressor reasonably near the relay, or the connections just won't reach. It's normal for the manufacturers to specify a certain way up for the compressor to be mounted, but there shouldn't be any other problems. You'll need to make sure that the electrical connections are as per the maker's instructions for the relay and compressor, and decide whether you want to use the air horns in conjunction with, or in place of, the original car horn. If you have to connect into existing wiring, make sure the connections are well made and, if these involve soldering, don't forget to insulate any soldered joints.

Hazard Warning

It's to be hoped that you'll never break down on a busy road or in an awkward spot, but if it does happen then it's reassuring to have a hazard warning system fitted. This is a device which enables all four direction indictor lamps to flash simultaneously to warn other vehicles that you're stationary and to help them spot you in bad visibility – not (despite frequent use for the purpose) to indicate that you've parked on double yellow lines to pop into the tobacconists's! Full instructions are supplied with these kits, but wiring can be tricky as a number of connections have to be made into existing circuits.

Child Safety Seats and Harness

Much has been said in recent years about the use of seat belts for front seat passengers, and more recently there's been an increasing interest in the various special rear seats and harnesses now available, for young children. It's very difficult to give any precise instructions for fitting these, because there are so many types around, but what you must be careful about is ensuring that you buy a BSI-approved type.

Most types have a pair of straps at the lower edge which need to be attached to the rear seat pan at the back of the squab, and a further pair of straps that fit over the back of the car seat for attachment to the rear parcel shelf (or the floor or wheel arch with estate cars). Take very careful note of the manufacturer's instructions; they require the anchorages to be a certain distance apart, and may also require reinforcing plates to be used.

Before starting to drill holes for the mountings, make sure the underside or rear of the panel's clear of obstructions, pipes or any other components. It may also be possible to utilise existing tapped fitting points. If in doubt, get in touch with the seat or harness manufacturers – they'll be only too pleased to give advice.

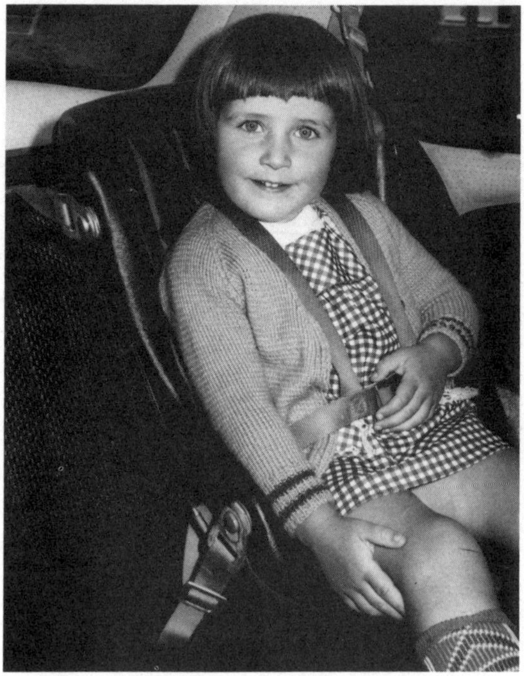

KL's Jeenay child safety seat

Lamps

When auxiliary lamps are fitted, not only must you fit them in a suitable place on the car, but that place must also meet certain legal requirements; Where these apply we've attempted to give some guidelines.

In addition to the actual lights themselves, we have to think of the switches (not normally difficult because many small switch panels are available, or you may already have a console which will take them, or you can simply drill a hole in a suitable spot on the dash panel), fusing, cable sizes, and whether relays are necessary.

Spot and fog lamps

It's illegal to mount these with their centres *more than* 3 ft 6 in (1067 mm) from the ground. Any lamps that are mounted with their centres *less than* 2 ft (610 mm) above the ground may only be used in fog or falling snow, and a single lamp may be used only *in conjunction with* headlamps. The lamps must always be mounted and used in pairs (two fog, two spot, or one of each) if they're to be used independently of the headlights. Their inner edges must be *not less than* 13·8 in (350 mm) apart and their outer edges must be *within* $15\frac{3}{4}$ in (400 mm) off the edge of the car. If they're used as spotlamps, they must conform to the normal anti-dazzle requirements, by wiring them via the dip switch or by pointing them slightly downwards.

Choose the lamps carefully, and if possible match the lamp styles. There are many good types on sale, so if you're not sure what you want seek some advice. Vauxhall dealers can offer you a pair of matched halogen foglamps (one pencil beam and one spread beam) in stainless steel, together with a kit to fit to the bumper brackets.

To prevent overload of the switch or wiring, a relay should be used (the Lucas 6RA type, part no. 33213 is suitable). This is connected through the switch from the existing headlamp circuit to one of the relay 'coil' terminals, the other going to a good earth point. The lamp wires then go to one of the relay 'contact' terminals, with the other terminal going either to the battery or the battery terminal on the starter solenoid via an in-line fuse. The fuse rating will depend on the lamp manufacturer's recommendations, but will probably be about 20 amps for both lamps. A good place to mount the relay is fairly near the starter solenoid and battery, to reduce the cable runs to a minimum.

Reversing lamps

If your Viva's not already fitted with reversing lamps, then Vauxhall can supply a kit consisting of either one or two flush-fitting lamps and a switch for automatic operation.Provision's made for the reversing light switch on the gearbox; this is much preferable to any dash-mounted type. Cable from lamp to switch should be run through the car floor if possible and under the carpet, but don't forget to use grommets or the holes which you've drilled will cut through the cable insulation.

The flush-mounted lamps are the neatest type to fit, and they'll go on the rear panel beneath the bumper. You'll need to drill holes for the mounting screws, and any holes for the leads will need grommets. Don't forget that it you're not using the gearbox actuated switch, any other type must have a warning light wired in parallel with the reverse light. An in-line fuse will be needed, probably about 10 amps rating, but it will depend on the actual lamp(s) used.

Rear fog lights

These can be mounted in much the same way as reversing lamps, although bumper-mounting types are very popular and these are the kind supplied as a Vauxhall-approved accessory. For wiring, the same sort of instructions apply as for separately switched reversing lamps (in fact some types serve a dual function in having a clear lens for reversing and a red snap-on lens for the fog light). If you're using the Vauxhall lamps there's a special switch/warning lamp kit available, which can be connected to your front fog lamps as well.

Anti-Theft Devices

There are three main categories of car thieves – those people who want your car either as a complete item or for the major mechanical and body parts; those who are out for a joy-ride; and those who merely want the contents. With any type of thief it makes sense to do what you can to deter someone from *wanting* to get in; don't leave valuables lying about, don't leave the car unlocked, and, if it's parked at home, put it in a locked garage if possible. But, if a car thief decides he does want your particular car, statistically he's got a pretty good chance of getting it!

All later cars have a steering column lock which is a very effective protection against a car being driven away, but it still makes sense to have a good burglar alarm fitted. Many types are available, and many of these are wired into door courtesy light switches or hidden switches beneath seats. Other types are wired into the horn circuit, but separate horns and bells are available; the more unconventional it is (whilst still being reliable) the better. Don't put hidden switches in the first place you think of – it might be the first place the thief thinks of too!

Some anti-theft devices are activated by the movement caused through somebody trying to get into the car (and occasionally by an innocent passerby!). Some not only sound alarms, but also earth the ignition circuit; other devices simply mechanically lock together the steering wheel and brake pedal. Have a look round the accessory shops and see what suits your car, your pocket and the degree of protection required.

Radios and Tape Players

A radio or tape player's an expensive item to buy, and will only give its best performance if fitted properly. It's useless to expect concert hall performance from a unit that's suspended from the dash panel by string with its speaker resting on the back seat or parcel shelf! If you don't want to do the installation yourself there are many in-car entertainment specialists who can do the fitting for you.

Make sure the unit purchased is of the same polarity as the car, or that units with adjustable polarity are correctly set before commencing installation.

It's difficult to give specific information about fitting, as final positioning of the radio/tape player, speakers, and aerial is entirely a matter of your personal preference. However, the following paragraphs give guidelines to follow, relevant to all installations.

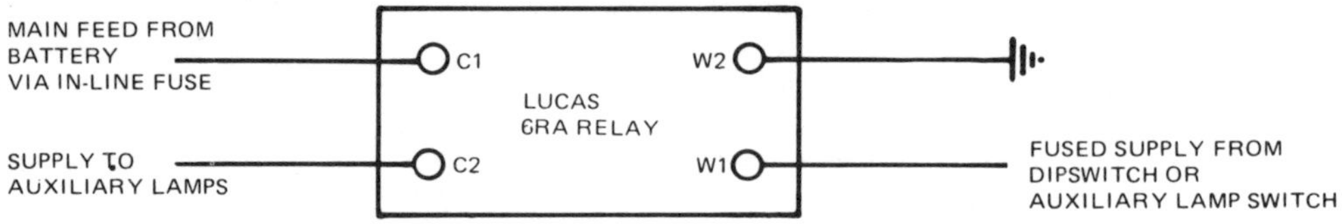

Connections for auxiliary lamps using a relay

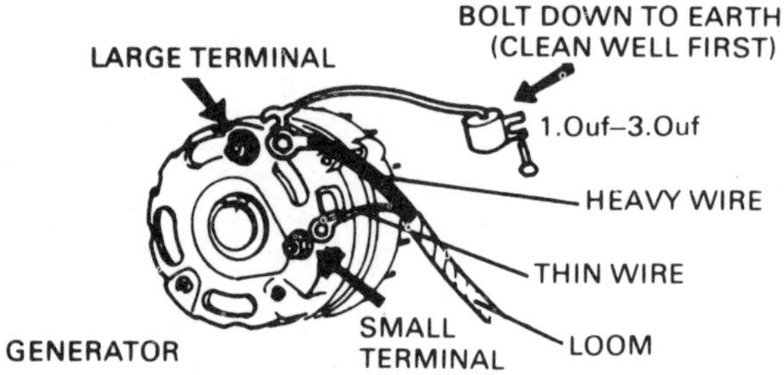

The correct way to connect a capacitor to the generator

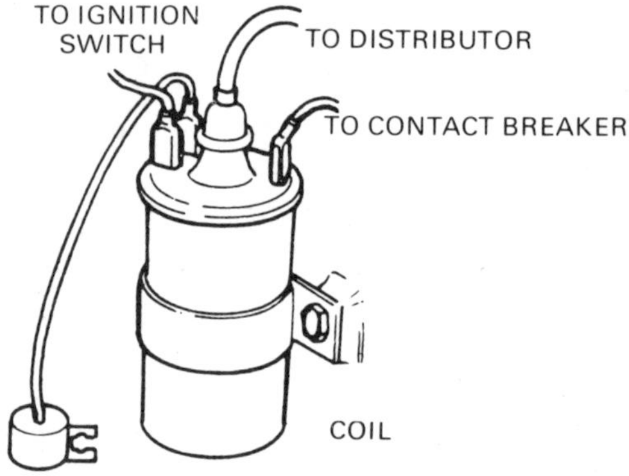

The correct way to connect a capacitor to the coil

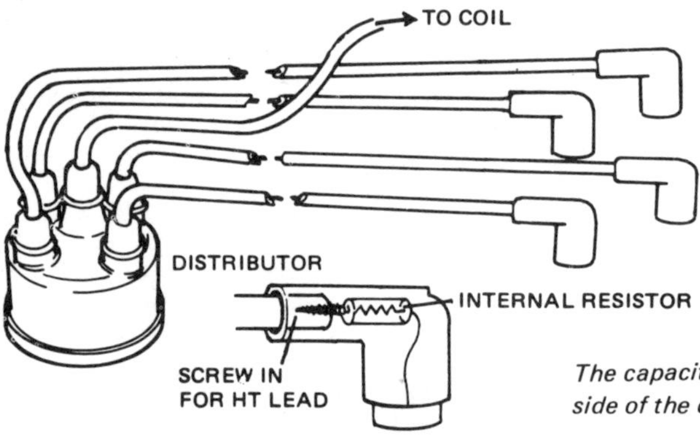

The capacitor must be connected to the ignition switch side of the coil

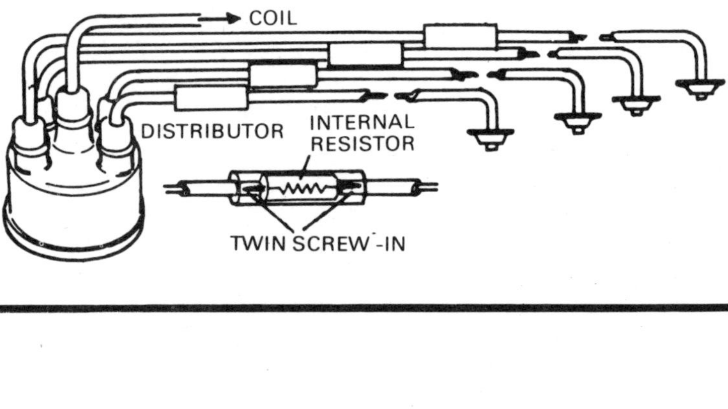

Ignition HT lead suppressors

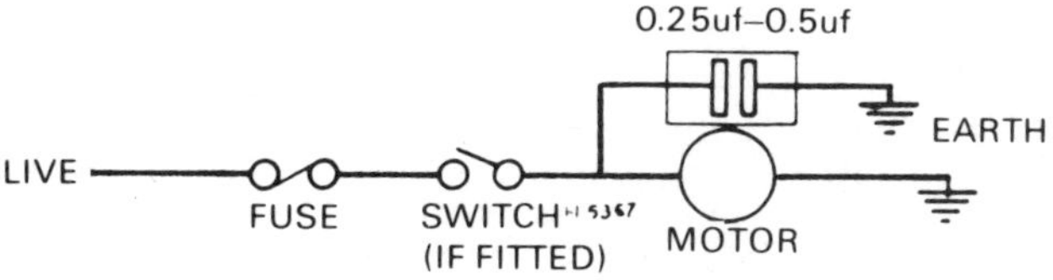

The correct way to suppress electric motors which are causing interference

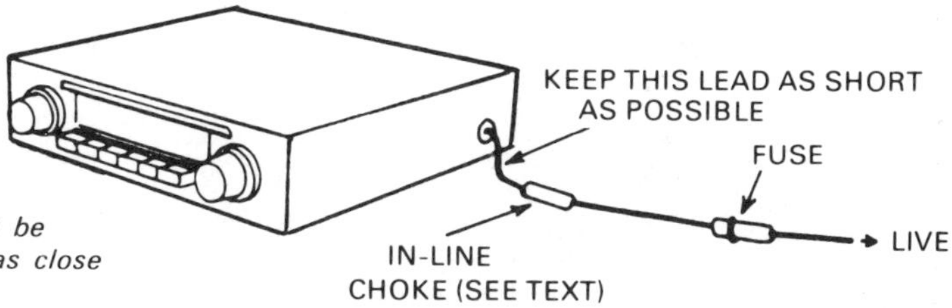

An in-line choke should be fitted in the feed wire as close to the unit as possible

Radios

Most radios are a standardised size of 7 inches wide, by 2 inches deep – this ensures that they'll fit into the radio aperture provided in many cars. On most Vivas a radio has to be fitted centrally under the facia, but the following points should be borne in mind before deciding exactly where to fit the unit:

a) It should be within easy reach of the driver wearing a seat belt.
b) It shouldn't be mounted close to an electric tachometer, the ignition switch and its wiring, or the flasher unit and associated wiring.
c) It should be mounted within reach of the aerial lead (you can use an extension cable if necessary) and in such a place that the aerial lead won't have to be routed near the components detailed in 'b'.
d) It shouldn't be positioned in a place where it might cause injury to the car occupants in an accident; for instance, under the dash panel above the driver's or passenger's legs.
e) It should be fitted really securely.

The type of aerial used, and where you're going to fit it, is a matter of personal preference. In general, the taller the aerial, the better the reception but there are limits to what's practicable. If you can, fit a fully retractable type – it saves an awful lot of problems with vandals and car wash equipment. When choosing a suitable spot for the aerial, remember the following points:

a) The aerial lead should be as short as possible.
b) The aerial should be mounted as far away from the distributor and HT leads as possible.
c) The part of the aerial which protrudes beneath the mounting point must not foul the roadwheels, or anything else.
d) If possible the aerial should be positioned so that the lead does not have to be routed through the engine compartment.
e) The areial should be mounted at a more-or-less vertical angle.

Again it should be mentioned that a full range of radios and cassette players, plus ordinary and electrically-operated aerials, is available through Vauxhall dealers.

Radio interference suppression

Books have been written on the subject, so we're not going to be able to tell you a lot in this small space. To reduce the possibility of your radio picking up unwanted interference, an in-line choke should be fitted in the feed wire and the set itself must be earthed really securely. The next step is to start connecting capacitors to reduce the amount of interference being generated by the different circuits of the car's electrics. The accompanying illustrations show the various interference generators and give capacitor values for the suppressors. When it comes to the ignition HT leads, these are resistors which can either be suppressor-type plug caps or in-line suppressors; if you're already using resistive HT leads (those with the carbon fibre filling), they're already doing the job for you.

Tape players

Fitting instructions for both cartridge and cassette stereo tape players are the same and in general the same rules apply as when fitting a radio. Tape players aren't usually prone to electrical interference like radios – although it can occur – so positioning isn't so critical. If possible the player should be mounted on an even keel. Also, it must be possible for a driver wearing a seat belt to reach the unit in order to change or turn over tapes.

Visibility Aids

Mirrors

Recent EEC legislation has done wonders for the looks of exterior mirrors. In additional to being functional, they now must have no projections to catch clothing or other cars, and must fold flat when struck. The result is a new wave of products in all shapes and sizes, some of which can be sprayed to match up with the existing car finish. There has also been a marked swing recently from wing mirrors to the door mounting kind, and these are available in the official Vauxhall accessory range, to fit either side of the car.

Choose mirrors which you think will suit the car's styling and, having got them, select the mounting point carefully. You'll get a good idea of where the best place is by simply looking at other cars, but get someone to hold the mirror while you sit in the driving seat just to make sure you can see all you need to.

Mark the position on the wing or door, and if you're fitting two mirrors do likewise on the other to make sure they're both in the same position. Check the hole size needed and, if you can, select a drill this size, plus, where applicable, a smaller one to make a pilot hole. If you haven't got the large drill required for most wing mirrors, you'll have to drill several small holes and file them out to the correct size.

Don't forget to remove any burrs from the hole afterwards, then paint on a little primer to cover the bare metal edges. When the primer's dry you can fit the mirror following the maker's instructions, then angle it as necessary to get the best rear view.

Rear window demisters

At one time, if you car wasn't fitted with a heated rear window as standard equipment (and only the expensive models were) about the only remedy was a

MAG 'European' door mirror

stick-on clear panel designed to act a bit like double glazing. They didn't usually work very well and frequently came unstuck too. Now they've been more or less superseded by the element type of stick-on demister. These act more like the genuine article, consisting of a metal foil element which is peeled off a backing sheet and stuck on to the inside surface of the rear window glass. It has to be wired up to the electrical system, of course, via a suitable fuse and switch, using sufficiently heavy cable and preferably incorporating a warning lamp as it will take quite a large current and shouldn't be left on inadvertently. The great thing about these devices is that they do work and are very moderately priced.

Rear window wipe/wash

This applies more to the Estate version of the 1100/1300 but can be very useful where it's found that the back window regularly becomes obscured by road dirt from the car's slipstream in wet weather.

Fitting may be found to be beyond the scope of the ordinary owner because the wiper motor has to be fitted into the inside 'skin' of the tailgate. The wiring and washer tubing, too, is slightly complicated by having to be passed through the whole length of the body from the switch/reservoir before being led through into the tailgate. Again, full instructions will be supplied by the makers, if you're prepared to have a go!

Headlamp conversions

Still on the subject of better visibility, if your problem's seeing in the dark, then you might well consider uprating your car's headlamps. A number of conversions are available for the standard British 7-inch units fitted to the HA models, and for the rectangular lamps on the later cars uprated bulbs can be obtained. Mostly they're fitted by simply interchanging with the old ones, no wiring modifications being needed (see *In An Emergency* for headlight removal).

Comfort

Longer journeys can be much more pleasant if your car's comfortable to drive, and just a couple of suggestions on this theme may be welcome.

Sound reducing kits

Very few cars have yet been produced in which the noise level, particularly at motorway speeds, is all that could be desired. For economy reasons, most manufacturers put only a certain amount of underfelt and sound-deadening material into their cars, and a further improvement can usually be made by fitting one of the proprietary kits. These are usually tailored to fit individual models, and consist of sections of felt-like material which are glued in place under carpets, inside hollow sections, boot lid etc, in accordance with instructions. The material can also be bought in rolls for D-I-Y cutting, using the carpets etc as templates.

Seats

If your car seats are showing signs of old age (and just fitting new covers won't disguise the sagging when you sit in them) then you can of course have them rebuilt by an upholstery specialist. On the other hand, if you agree that the seats in the Viva models aren't the most comfortable ever made, you could think about replacing at least the driver's seat by one of the special bucket types available. To look at these you'll have to find an accessory shop stocking the more motor sport orientated kind of goods.

Miscellaneous

Electronic ignition

Such systems are many and varied and widely advertised. The makers claim easier starting, better performance and lower fuel consumption as the main advantages, and on the whole these claims are substantiated in practice. However, before buying one of the available kits we suggest you stop and reflect whether your mileage and type of driving makes the expenditure worthwhile. Get other advice, preferably from someone who's fitted such a system to his own car. Consider too whether you're capable of installing it yourself, otherwise you'll have to pay for fitting as as well.

There are several types of electronic ignition – some retain the conventional contact-breaker in the car's distributor while others replace this by a magnetic triggering device. Even where the contact points are retained they're no longer likely to burn and therefore shouldn't need replacing so frequently – but this doesn't in itself amount to much of a saving.

Roof racks

Many an owner has to resort to a luggage rack from time to time, even if it's only for family holidays. The types available are very varied, but they normally rely on clips attached to the water drain channel above the doors. If you're buying, select a size that suits your requirements, making sure that it's not too wide for the roof!

When fitting the roof rack, position it squarely on the roof, preferably towards the front rather than the rear. After it's loaded, by the way, recheck the tension of the attachment bracket screws.

MAG Universal dog guard

Don't keep the roof rack on when it's not wanted; it offers too much wind resistance and creates a surprising amount of noise (see *Save It!*).

Dog/Luggage guards

Owners of Estate versions of the Viva who either own a dog or carry large loads in the rear of the vehicle will no doubt find one of these tubular barriers beneficial. They're normally adjustable telescopically, both for height and width, and are fitted by clamping between roof and load deck immediately behind the rear seat to keep dog, luggage or whatever in its rightful place and possibly prevent injury to the front seat occupants in an emergency stop.

Mudflaps

You're probably already aware that both front and rear wheel arches can be fitted with mudflaps. These will not only protect your car's underside and paintwork from flying stones, but will also earn the thanks of following drivers owing to the reduction in spray during wet weather. Fitting's straightforward and is usually by means of clamping brackets or self-tapping screws. Vauxhall dealers can supply tailor-made ones with a fitting kit.

Specialist Fitments

We've now covered a lot of main items likely to interest the average owner from the D-I-Y fitting angle. Such things as towbars and sunshine or vinyl roofs, while practical or desirable, are beyond the scope both of this book and of the ordinary car owners. We therefore recommend that for any major accessory of this kind you consult the appropriate specialist who'll be able to give you an initial estimate of the cost as well as carrying out the work properly and safely.

Troubleshooting

We've gone to great lengths in this book to provide as much information on your car as we think you'll need for satisfactory running and D-I-Y servicing. Hopefully, you won't need to use this chapter but there's always a possibility (rather than a probability!) that something will go wrong, and by reference to the charts which follow you should be able to pinpoint the trouble even if you can't actually fix it yourself.

The charts are broken down into the main systems of the car and, where there's a fairly straightforward remedy – the sort you can tackle yourself – **bold type** is used to highlight it. Further information on that particular item will normally be found elsewhere in the Handbook; look up the component or system in the Index to find the correct page. In some cases a reference number will be found (e.g. T1/1); by looking up this number in the accompanying Cross-reference Table, you'll find more information on that particular fault.

TROUBLESHOOTER 1:

Starter motor doesn't work when key is turned

- **Flat battery (T1/1)**
  Battery connections loose or corroded
  Loose connection to starter (T1/2)
  Automatic transmission selector not at 'N'
- Starter motor or solenoid switch faulty internally

Starter motor doesn't work properly

- Turns engine very slowly
  - **Battery flat (T1/1)** or defective
    Internal starter motor fault
  - **Spark plug lead(s) loose, disconnected, damp or faulty (T1/4)**
    Spark plugs dirty, cracked or incorrectly gapped.
    Distributor or coil cap damp, cracked or HT lead loose.
    Worn distributor cap electrodes.
    Coil or condenser faulty (T1/5).
    Contact breaker points dirty or incorrectly set.
    Ignition timing incorrect.
- Doesn't turn engine
  - **Starter pinion sticking (T1/3)**

ENGINE — STARTING

Works noisily or harshly

- Pinion or flywheel teeth broken or worn.
- Starter drive main spring broken. **Starter motor retaining bolts loose (T1/7)**

Starter motor turns engine normally but engine won't start

Ignition system fault

Spark plug lead(s) loose, disconnected or damp (T1/4).
Spark plugs dirty, cracked or incorrectly gapped.
Distributor or coil cap cracked or HT lead loose.
Worn distributor cap electrodes.
Coil or condenser faulty (T1/5).
Contact breaker points dirty or incorrectly set.
Ignition timing incorrect.

Fuel system fault

Fuel pump faulty or fuel line disconnected.
Leak in fuel pump or fuel lines.
Carburettor float chamber fuel level incorrect.
Carburettor incorrectly set.
Choke not operating correctly.

Air cleaner blocked.
Valve clearances incorrect.
Inlet manifold or gasket or carburettor gasket leaking.
Brake servo hose leaking (if fitted) (T1/8).
Engine flooded (excess fuel).
Engine seriously overheated (T1/9).

TROUBLESHOOTER 2:

Lacks Power

Ignition fault
Timing incorrect

Fuel system fault

Other causes

Incorrect valve clearances.
Low cylinder compression
Air cleaner blocked.

Overheating

Insufficient water in cooling system/leakage from system (T2/1).
Fan belt slipping.
Radiator blocked or grille obstructed (T2/2).
Water hose collapsed or kinked (T2/3).
Thermostat not operating properly.
Exhaust system obstructed or damaged.
Blown cylinder head gasket.
Engine not yet run-in (T2/4).
Brakes binding (Table 4).
Oil level too low.

Running too cool

Incorrect thermostat installed
Thermostat missing or not working properly.

Misfires

Ignition fault

ENGINE — RUNNING

Cuts Out Unexpectedly

Fuel system fault

Ignition fault
Water on ignition components (T1/4).
Coil or condenser failed.
LT lead to coil or distributor disconnected.
HT lead from coil loose or disconnected.

Fuel system fault
Tank empty.
Fuel pump faulty.
Fuel line broken, leaking or blocked.

Spark plug lead(s) loose, disconnected, damp or faulty (T1/4).
Spark plugs dirty, cracked or incorrectly gapped.
Distributor or coil cap damp, cracked or HT lead loose.
Worn distributor cap electrodes.
Coil or condenser faulty (T1/5).
Contact breaker points dirty or incorrectly set.
Ignition timing incorrect.

Fuel pump faulty or **fuel line disconnected.**
Leak in fuel pump or fuel lines.
Carburettor float chamber fuel level incorrect.
Carburettor incorrectly set.

TROUBLESHOOTER 3:

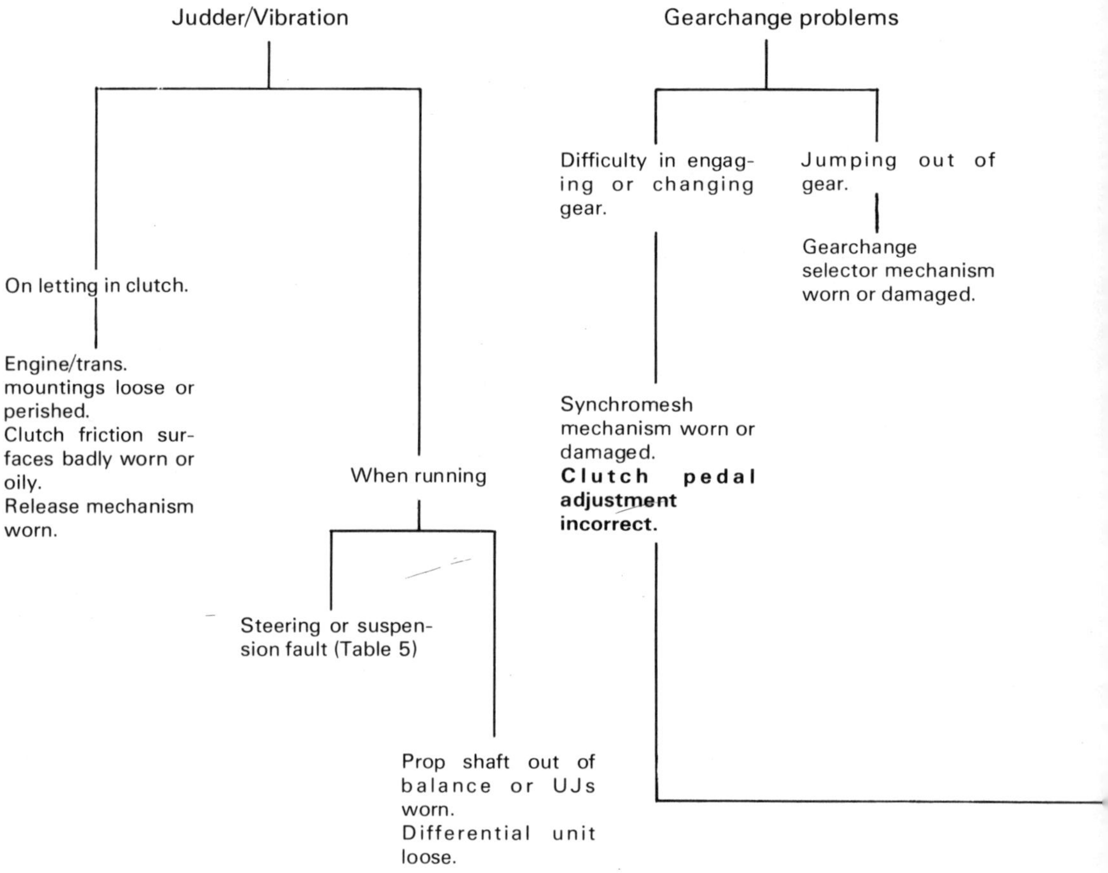

CLUTCH & TRANSMISSION

Irregular Noises

- From clutch
  - On depressing pedal.
    - Release mechanism dry, worn or damaged. **Pedal pivot requires lubrication.**
  - On releasing pedal.
    - Release mechanism dry, worn or damaged. **Pedal pivot requires lubrication.**
    - Clutch driven plate distorted.
- From gearbox.
  - Whining or grinding noise while running.
    - **Incorrect grade of oil in use or low level.** Gear teeth or bearings worn or damaged.
  - Crunching noises when changing gear.
    - Synchromesh mechanism worn or damaged. Clutch pedal adjustment incorrect.
- From differential.
  - Crownwheel and pinion incorrectly meshed or badly worn.

TROUBLESHOOTER 4:

Pedal Operation

- Excessive pedal travel
  - **Fluid level too low.**
    Rear brakes need adjusting
  - Leaks in system
    Wheel cylinder or caliper leaking.
    Master cylinder leaking.
    Brake line or hose leaking.
- 'Spongy' feel
  - Leaks in system
    Wheel cylinder or caliper leaking.
    Master cylinder leaking.
    Brake line or hose leaking.
  - Air in system (requires bleeding).
- 'Springy' feel or high pedal pressure needed.
  New linings/pads not yet bedded in.
  Drums/discs badly scored or distorted.
  Master cylinder bolts loose.
  Linings contaminated by dirt, oil, grease or fluid.
  Brake servo faulty or hose loose or damaged (T4/1).

TROUBLESHOOTER 5:

- Steering feels light and vague
  - Tyres
    Pressures too high.
    Wrong type.
  - Suspension geometry wrong.
  - Steering balljoints badly worn.
    Steering gear needs adjusting.
- Steering wheel has too much free play
  - Steering balljoints badly worn.
    Steering gear needs adjusting.
- Steering feels stiff and heavy
  - **Tyre pressures too low or uneven.**
    Suspension balljoints need greasing.
    Suspension geometry wrong.
    Steering gear over-adjusted.
    Steering columns badly distorted.

BRAKES

Effect on Car

Car pulls to one side

Drums/linings or pads/discs contaminated with oil, grease or fluid.
Brake backplate, caliper or disc loose.
Shoes or pads incorrectly fitted.
Differing types of linings fitted at each side.
Suspension anchorages loose.
Drums/discs badly worn or distorted.
Tyre pressures unequal.

Brakes 'grab' or wheel(s) lock.

Contamination by oil, grease or fluid.

Brakes bind when pedal released.

Rear brakes/handbrake over-adjusted.
Master cylinder pushrod out of adjustment.
Vent hole in reservoir cap blocked.
Master cylinder or wheel cylinder seized.

STEERING & SUSPENSION

Wobble/vibration from front wheels

Loose wheelnuts.
Damaged wheel.
Wheels/tyres need balancing.
Steering/suspension balljoints worn.

Car settles too low or leans to one side while stationary

Weak springs.

Car leans over excessively when cornering

Weak springs.
Worn shock absorbers.
Low tyre pressures.

TROUBLESHOOTER 6:

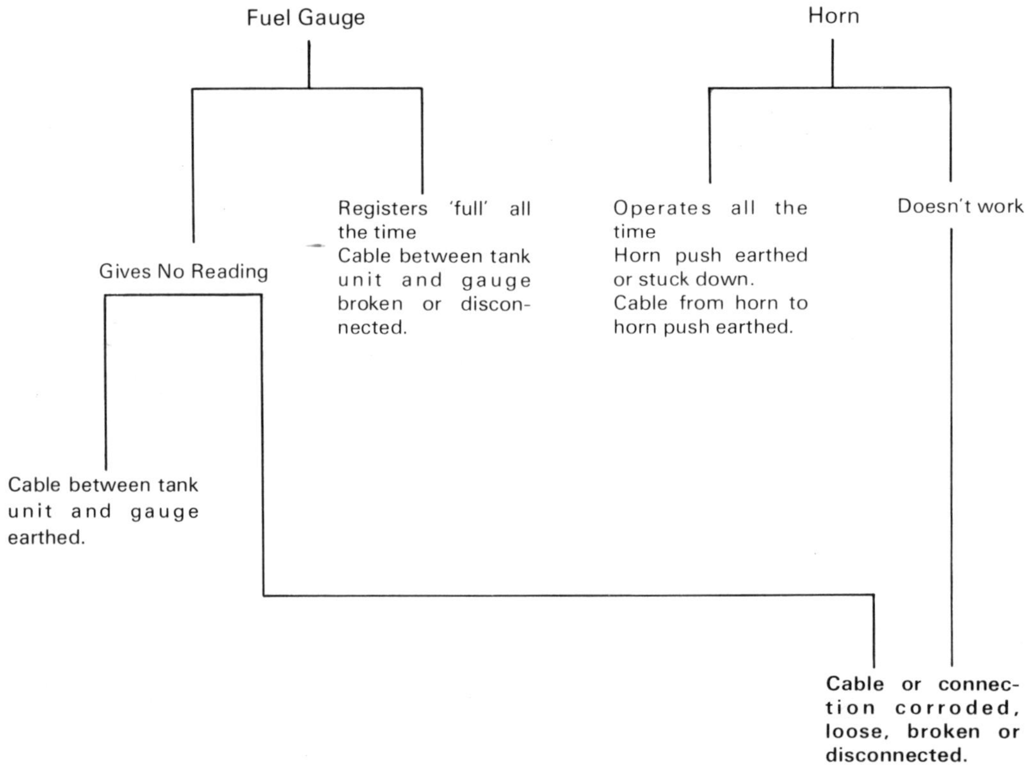

Note: This chart assumes that the battery installed in your car is in good condition and of the correct specification, and that the terminal connections are clean and tight. A car used frequently for stop-start motoring or for short journeys (particularly during the winter when lights, heater blower etc are likely to be in use) may need its battery recharged at intervals to keep it serviceable. If an electrical problem occurs, don't immediately suspect the starter or any other component without first checking that the battery's capable of supplying its needs.

ELECTRICS

Lights

- Don't come on or Come on but go out again
  - **Battery flat.**
    Bulb or filament broken.
    Light switch faulty.
  - Light switch faulty.
- Work erratically or flicker on and off.
  - Light switch faulty.
  - **Lamps not earthing properly (T6/1).**
- Give very poor illumination.
  Bulbs or lenses dirty or corroded.
  Wrong bulbs installed.

A fault occurring in any other electrical equipment or accessory not specifically referred to above can usually be traced to one of three main causes i.e. Blown fuse; loose or broken connection to power supply or earth; or internal fault in the equipment.

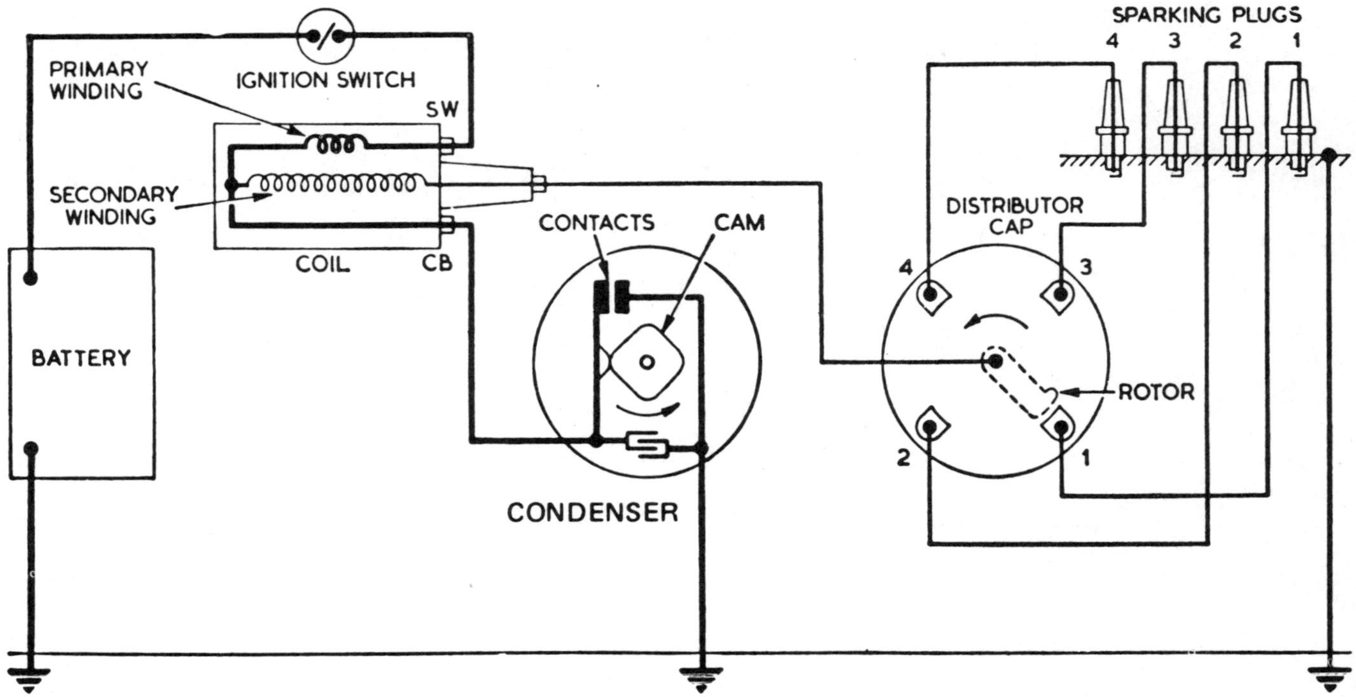

The ignition circuit – LT system indicated by heavier lines

CROSS-REFERENCE TABLE

TROUBLESHOOTER REFERENCE	ADDITIONAL INFORMATION
T1/1	Either charge the battery from a battery charger, or use jumper leads to start the car from another battery, make sure that the lead polarities are correct in both cases, or you may do permanent damage, particularly if your car has an alternator.
T1/2	If the lead's loose, disconnect the battery earth lead then tighten the connection on the starter motor; Make sure the bolt doesn't turn while you're tightening the nut. Reconnect the battery earth lead.
T1/3	You can use a spanner on the square-ended shaft on the end of the starter motor. By turning it you'll normally be able to free it from the ring gear.
T1/4	Make sure that all the connections are tight, then wipe the leads clean and dry with a lint-free cloth. Use an ignition system waterproofer (e.g. WD40 or Damp Start) to prevent problems in the future.
T1/5	An ignition coil is a simple item to fit, but make a note of the connections before removing them, and ensure that the replacement coil's the correct type. Renewal of the condenser (the small cylindrical object attached to the distributor) is equally easy – just note the connections before removing.
T1/6	To check the operation of the pump, detach the fuel outlet pipe (that's the one that goes to the carburettor) and turn the engine on the starter a few times; there should be a steady stream of petrol if the pump's working properly. Cleaning the fuel pump filter is covered in the 6000-mile Service Schedule.
T1/7	It's easy enough to tighten the attachment bolts if you've got a box or socket spanner of the right size; if you haven't, it's not really a D-I-Y job.
T1/8	For a temporary repair a leaking hose can normally be bound up with adhesive tape or, better still, with a hose bandage available for the purpose.
T1/9	Wait till the system's cooled down, then top it up. If it happens a second time, get it looked at straight away or you could ruin your engine (if it hasn't happened already). If it's just a leaking hose you can probably bind it up as in T1/8 (above) to get yourself home.
T2/2	Driving carefully will probably get you home. An airline on the radiator core will clean out the dirt that's accumulated; if it's blocked internally use a proprietary flushing compound.
T2/3	You may be able to repair the hose temporarily (see T1/8) but it'll almost certainly mean a new one.
T2/4	Drive more slowly – but without labouring the engine.
T4/1	Provided there's no loss of hydraulic fluid, you'll need a little extra pedal effort for braking but that's all. It may be possible to temporarily repair the hose as in T1/8.
T6/1	Remove the lamp lenses (see *In An Emergency)* and check for signs of rust. Where there's rust, scrape it off and apply a little Vaseline. Ensure that the screws securing the lamp body to the car are making good contact.

Car Jargon Explained

We hope there isn't much in this Handbook that you can't understand. However, most of us – particularly if we're trying to learn more about an unfamiliar subject – will sooner or later come across the odd word or phrase that needs explaining. This alphabetical list should help you understand the language spoken by your garage man, 'expert' neighbour, or that inevitable chap in the local ...

A

Accelerator pump: A device attached to many *carburettors* which adds a spurt of extra fuel to the carburettor mixture when the accelerator pedal is suddenly pressed down.

AF: An abbreviation of 'across flats, the way in which many nuts, bolt heads and spanners are now identified. It's preceded by an Imperial or metric unit of measurement – e.g. $\frac{1}{2}$ in AF or 11 mm AF.

Additives: Compounds which are added to petrol and lubricating oil to improve their quality and performance.

Advance and retard: A system for altering the ignition timing – the time in the firing cycle at which the ignition spark occurs. The spark timing is normally a few degrees of *crankshaft* revolution before the *piston* reaches the top of its stroke, and is expressed as so many degrees before top-dead-centre (BTDC). It's altered by devices in the *distributor* which detect changes in engine speed and load. Broadly speaking, as the engine speeds up the ignition is advanced (greater angle BTDC) but if there is a heavy engine load the ignition is retarded (smaller angle BTDC).

Air cooling: Alternative method of engine cooling in which no water is used. An engine-driven fan forces air at high velocity over the engine surfaces, which are enclosed by cowling. Normally an *oil cooler* is incorporated in the air flow to assist the rate of heat loss.

Alternator: A device for converting rotating mechanical energy into electrical energy. In modern cars, it has superseded the *dynamo* for charging the battery because of its much greater efficiency.

Ammeter: A device for measuring the current supplied to the battery from the *dynamo* or *alternator*, or drawn from the battery by the car lights, wipers, radio etc.

Anti-dive: Characteristic of a *suspension* designed to prevent the car adopting a nose-down attitude during heavy braking.

Antifreeze: A chemical compound mixed with the cooling system water to lower the temperature at which the coolant freezes.

Anti-roll bar: A spring-steel bar mounted transversely across a car which counteracts the nautral tendency for the car to lean over when cornering.

Anti-squat: Characteristic of a *suspension* designed to prevent the car adopting a nose-up attitude during acceleration.

Aquaplaning: A phrase used to describe the action of a tyre skating across water.

Automatic transmission: A type of *gearbox* which selects the correct gear ratio automatically according to the engine speed and load.

B

Balljoint: A ball-and-socket type joint, used in steering and *suspension* systems, which permits relative movement in more than one plane.

Battery condition indicator: A voltmeter connected via the ignition switch to the car battery. Unlike an *ammeter* (which it's tending to supersede), it will warn you of impending battery failure.

Bearing: Metal or other hard wearing surface against which another part moves or rotates, and which is designed (and usually lubricated) to withstand the resulting friction.
Bendix drive: A device on many types of starter motor which allows the motor to be coupled to the *flywheel* for engine starting, then disengages when the engine commences to run.
BHP: See *Horsepower.*
Big end: The end of a *connecting rod* which is attached to the *crankshaft.* It incorporates a *bearing* and transmits the linear movement of the con-rod into the rotary motion of the crankshaft.
Bleed nipple (or valve): A hollow screw with a tapered seat which allows air or fluid to be bled out of a system when it is loosened.
Brake caliper: That part of a *disc brake* system which houses the *brake pads* and the *hydraulic* operating *pistons.*
Brake fade: A temporary loss of braking efficiency due to overheating of the brake friction material.
Brake pad: That part of a *disc brake* system which comprises the friction material and a metal backing plate.
Brake shoe: That part of a *drum brake* system which comprises the friction material and a curved metal former.
Breather: A device which allows fresh air into a system or allows contaminated air out.
Bucket tappet: A cup (or bucket) shaped piece of metal used in some engines to transmit the rotary *camshaft* movement to an up-and-down movement for *valve* operation.
Bump stop: A hard rubber device used in many *suspension* systems to prevent the moving parts from lifting the bodyframe during violent suspension movements.

C

Camber angle: The angle at which the front wheels are set from the vertical, when viewed from the front of the car. Positive camber is the amount in degrees by which the wheels are tilted outwards at the top.
Cam follower: A cylindrical piece of metal used to transmit the rotary *camshaft* movement to an up-and-down movement for *valve* operation.
Camshaft: A rotating shaft with lobes or cams used to operate the engine *valves.*
Carbon fibre leads: Black, string-like cores in the centre of some spark plug *HT* leads, which don't need separate radio and *TV* suppressors.
Carburettor: A device which is used to mix air and fuel in the correct proportions for all conditions of engine running. There are two main types: those with a number of fixed *jets,* and those with a single jet with a moving needle in it. In the former type, the different jets come into operation at different conditions of throttle opening, engine speed and engine load; in the latter type, the *needle jet* is controlled by a moving *piston,* the position of which depends on the amount of suction in the engine inlet *manifold.*
Castor angle: The angle between the front wheel pivot points and a vertical line when viewed from the side of the car. Positive castor is when the axis is inclined rearwards.
Centrifugal advance: System of ignition *advance and retard* incorporated in many *distributors* in which weights rotating on a shaft alter the ignition timing according to engine speed.
Choke: This has two common meanings. It is used to describe the device which shuts off some of the air in a *carburettor* during cold starting, and may be either manually or automatically operated. It's also used as a general term to describe the carburettor throttle bore.
Clutch: A friction device which allows two rotating devices to be coupled together smoothly, without the need for either rotating part to stop.
Coil spring: A spiral of spring steel used in many *suspension* systems.
Combustion chamber: Shaped area in the *cylinder head* into which the fuel/air mixture is compressed by the *piston* and in which combustion of the mixture is effected by the *spark plug.*
Compression ratio (CR): A term used to describe the amount by which the fuel/air mixture is compressed, and expressed as a number. For example, an 8.5 : 1 compression ratio means that the volume of fuel/air when the *piston* is at the bottom ot its stroke is 8.5 times that when the piston is at the top of its stroke.
Compression tester: A special type of pressure gauge screwed into the *spark plug* hole which shows the *cylinder* compression when the engine is turning but not firing.
Condenser (capacitor): A device in the *distributor* which stores electrical energy and prevents excessive sparking at the *contact breaker* points.
Connecting rod (con-rod): Rod in the engine connecting the *piston* to the *crankshaft.*
Constant velocity (CV) joint: A joint used in *driveshafts,* where the speed of the input shaft is exactly the same as the speed of the output shaft at any angle of rotation. This does not occur in ordinary *universal joints.*
Contact breaker: The device in the *distributor* which comprises the electrical points (or contacts), and a

cam which opens and closes them to operate the *HT* electrical circuit which provides the spark at the *spark plug.*

Crossflow cylinder head: A *cylinder head* in which the inlet and exhaust *valves* are on opposite sides.

Crossply tyre: A tyre whose construction is such that the weave of the fabric material layers is running diagonally in alternatively opposite directions to a line around the circumference.

Cubic capacity: The total volume within the *cylinders* which is swept by the *pistons.*

Cylinder head: That part of the engine which contains the *valves* and associated operating gear.

D

DIN: This stand for Deutsche Industrie Norm (roughly equivalent to the British Standards Institution) and lays down international standards for measuring output, performance, etc., of motor vehicles.

Damper:See *shock* absorber.

Dashpot: An oil-filled *cylinder* and *piston* used as a damping device in SU and Zenith/Stromberg CD type *carburettors.*

Dead axle (beam axle): The simplest form of axle, comprising a horizontal member attached to the chassis-frame by springs. This is used for the rear axle on some front-wheel-drive cars.

Decarobonizing ('decoking'): Removal of all carbon deposits from the *combustion chambers* of an engine.

De Dion axle: A rear axle comprising a cranked tube attached to the wheel hubs, with a separately mounted *differential* gear and *driveshafts. Suspension* is normally through *coil springs* between the wheel hubs and chassis frame.

Diaphragm: A stationary flexible membrane used in items such as fuel pumps. The diaphragm spring used in *clutches* is somewhat similar but is made from spring steel.

Diesel engine: An engine which relies upon the heat generated when compressing air to ignite the fuel, and which therefore doesn't need a *spark plug.* Diesel engines have much higher *compression ratios* than petrol engines, normally in the region of 20: 1.

Differential: A system of gears (generally known as a crownwheel and pinion) which allows the *torque* from the *propeller shaft* to be applied to the driving wheels. The torque is divided proportionately between the driving wheels to permit one wheel to turn faster than the other if required, for example during cornering.

Disc brake: A braking system where a rotating disc is clamped between hydraulically operated friction pads.

Distributor: A collective term used to described the *contact breaker, advance and retard* mechanisms, and associated parts of the *ignition system.*

Doughnut: A term used to describe the flexible rubber coupling used in some *driveshafts.*

Driveshaft: Name usually applied to the shaft (normally incorporating *universal* or *constant velocity joints*) which transmits the drive from a *transaxle* to one wheel; more commonly found in front-wheel-drive cars.

Drive train: A collective term used to described the *gearbox, propeller shaft, final drive* and *half-shafts* of a front engine/rear wheel drive car.

Drum brake: A brake with friction linings on 'shoes', running inside a cylindrical drum attached to the wheel.

Dual circuit brakes: A *hydraulic* braking system comprising two separate fluid circuits, so that if one circuit becomes inoperative, braking power is still available from the other circuit at a reduced efficiency.

Dwell angle: The number of degrees of *distributor* cam rotation during which the *contact breaker* points are closed during the ignition cycle of one *cylinder.* The angle is altered by adjusting the points gap, and is a more accurate way of setting-up the *ignition system.*

Dynamo: A device for converting rotating mechanical energy into electrical energy. This is a heavier, less efficient, form of *generator* than the *alternator*, and has largely been superseded by it during recent years.

E

Earth strap: A flexible electrical connection between the battery and vehicle earth, or the engine/*gearbox* and chassis frame, to provide the return current-flow path in the electrical system.

Electrode: An electrical terminal or terminals, across which a spark occurs e.g., in a *spark plug* or *distributor* cap.

Electrolyte: A current-conducting solution of water and sulphuric acid, which is the liquid inside the car battery.

Electronic ignition: An **ignition system** incorporating electronic components which can produce a much greater spark voltage than in conventional systems.

Emission control: The prevention or reduction of the emission into the atmosphere of noxious fumes and gases from the engine and fuel tank of a motor vehicle. Required to varying degrees by the laws of different countries, it is effected by design and by special devices.

Epicyclic gears (planetary gears): A gear system used in many *automatic transmissions* where there is a centre 'sun' wheel around which smaller 'planet' gears inside a 'planet carrier' rotate.

Exhaust gas analyser: An instrument used for the measurement of pollutants (mainly carbon monoxide) in an exhaust system.

Expansion tank: A container used in many modern cooling systems to collect the overflow from the car's *radiator* as the coolant heats up and expands.

F

Fastback: A term used to described a car by reference to its sloping rear shape.

Filter: A device for extracting foreign particles from air or oil.

Final drive: A collective term (often expressed as a gearing ratio) for the crownwheel and pinion (see *Differential).*

Flat engine: Form of engine design in which the *cylinders* are positioned horizontally, usually with an equal number each side of a central *crankshaft.*

Float chamber: That part of a *carburettor* which contains a float and *needle valve* for controlling the fuel level.

Flywheel: A heavy rotating disc attached to the *crankshaft* used to smooth out the pulsating output from the *cylinders.*

Four stroke (cycle): A common term used to described the four operating strokes of a *piston* in a conventional car engine. These are: (1) Induction – drawing in the fuel/air mixture as the piston goes down; (2) Compression of the fuel/air mixture as the piston rises; (3) Power stroke where the piston is forced down after the fuel/air mixture has been ignited by the *spark plug* and (4) Exhaust stroke where the piston rises and pushes the burnt gases out of the *cylinder.* During these operations, the inlet and exhaust *valves* are opened and closed at the correct moment to allow the fuel/air mixture in, the exhaust gases out, or to provide a gas-tight compression chamber.

Fuel injection: A method of injecting fuel into an engine. Used in *Diesel* engines, and also on some petrol engines as a replacement for the *carburettor.*

G

Gasket: Compressible material used between two metal surfaces to make a leak-proof joint.

Gearbox: A group of gears and shafts installed in a metal housing. Physically, this is positioned between the *clutch* and the *differential,* and is used to multiply the engine *torque.*

Generator: See *alternator* and *dynamo.*

GT: Gran Turismo (or sometimes Grand Touring); a term now loosely used to identify a saloon or fixed-head coupe style of car, with a high performance version of a normal production engine.

H

Half-shaft: A rotating shaft, two of which are used to transmit the drive from the *differential* to the wheels.

Hardy-Spicer joint (Hooke's or Cardan joint): See *Universal joint.*

Helical gears: Gears in which the teeth are cut at a slant across the circumference to give smoother meshing and quieter running.

Horsepower:A measurement of the rate of doing work. Where brake horsepower *(BHP)* is referred to, it's the amount of work required to stop a moving body.

HT: Abbreviation of high tension (meaning high voltage). Used on connection with the ignition system.

Hydragas suspension: *Suspension* system designed by Moulton Developments Ltd and fitted to the Austin Allegro. Similar in principle to *Hydrolastic* but with more effective damping, and gas springs in place of rubber cones.

Hydraulic: A term used to described the operation of a system by means of fluid pressure.

Hydrolastic suspension: A *suspension* system used on certain BLMC car models, in which fluid displaced in a unit by movement of one wheel is transferred to a similar unit at the other wheel on the same side. This helps to reduce pitching and rolling.

I

Ignition system: The electrical system which provides the spark to ignite the air/fuel mixture in the engine. Normally it comprises the battery, ignition coil, *distributor, (contact breaker and condenser),* ignition switch, *spark plugs* and wiring.

Ignition timing: See *Advance and retard.*

Inertia reel: Automatic type of safety belt which permits the wearer to move freely in normal use but which locks to give restraint on sensing either sudden deceleration of the car or sudden movement of the wearer.

In-line engine: Engine in which the *cylinders* are positioned in one row as distinct from being e.g. a *flat* or *vee* formation.

J

Jet: A calibrated nozzle or orifice in a *carburettor* through which fuel is drawn for mixing with air.
Jump leads: Heavy electric cables fitted with clips to enable a vehicle's battery to be connected to an external one for emergency starting.

K

Kerb weight: The weight of a car, unladen but ready to be driven, i.e. with enough fuel, oil etc. to travel an arbitrary distance.
Kickdown: A device used on *automatic transmissions* which allows a lower gear to be selected by flooring the accelerator.
Kingpin: A device which allows the front wheels of a car to swivel.

L

Laminated windscreen: A windscreen which has a thin plastic layer sandwiched between two layers of toughened glass. Its advantage is that it doesn't shatter or craze over when hit.
Leading shoe: Brake shoe of which the leading end (the one moved by the operating *cylinder)* is reached first by a given point on the drum during normal forward rotation. A simple single-cylinder *drum brake* will have one leading and one trailing (the opposite) shoe.
Leaf spring: A spring commonly used on cars with a *live axle,* comprising several long steel plates clamped together.
Little end: The smaller end of the *connecting rod* which is attached to the *piston.*
Live axle: An axle through which power is transmitted to the rear wheels.
Loom: A complete vehicle wiring system, or section thereof (e.g. front loom) comprising all the necessary cables of predetermined colours and lengths to wire up the various circuits.
LT: Abbreviation of low tension (meaning low voltage). Used in connection with *ignition systems.*

M

MacPherson strut: An independent front *suspension* system where the swivelling, springing and shock absorbing action of the wheel is dealt with by a single assembly.
Manifold: The device used for ducting the air/fuel mixture to the engine (inlet manifold), or the exhaust gases from the engine (exhaust manifold).

Master cylinder: A cylinder containing a *piston* and hydraulic fluid, directly coupled to a foot pedal (e.g. brake or clutch *master cylinder*). It's used for transmitting pressure to the brake or *clutch* operating mechanism.
Metallic paint: Paint finish incorporating minute particles of metal to give added lustre to the colour.
Multigrade: Lubricating oil whose *viscosity* covers that of several *monograde* oils, making it suitable for use over a wider range of operating conditions.

N

Needle bearing: Type of *bearing* in which needle or cone-shaped rollers are employed around the inner circumference, often used to reduce the space needed for the bearing.
Needle valve: A component of *carburettor* which restricts the flow of fuel or fuel/air mixture according to its position relative to an orifice or *jet.*
Negative earth: Electrical system (now almost universally adopted) in which the negative terminal of the car battery is connected to the vehicle body, the polarity of all other electrical equipment being determined by this.

O

Octane rating: A scale rating introduced by the British Standards Institution for grading petrol.
OHC (overhead cam): Describes an engine in which the *camshaft* is situated above the *cylinder head,* and operates the *valve* gear directly without the need for *pushrods.*
OHV (Overhead valve): Describes an engine which has its *valves* in the *cylinder head* (as in *OHC*) but suggests that the valve gear is operated via *pushrods* from a *camshaft* situated lower in the engine. Practically all modern car engines are OHV but are not necessarily OHC.
Oil cooler: Small *radiator* fitted in the lubricating oil circuit and sited in a cooling airflow to dissipate heat from the oil. Used mainly in higher-performance engines.
Overdrive: A device coupled to a car *gearbox* which raises the output gear ratio above the normal 1 : 1 of top gear. Also used to describe a top gear ratio of greater than 1 : 1 found in some cars.
Oversteer: A tendency for a car to turn more tightly into a corner than intended.

P

PCV (Positive crankcase ventilation): A system

which allows fumes and vapours which build up in the crankcase to be drawn into the engine for burning.

Pinion: A gear with a small number of teeth which meshes with one having a larger number of teeth.

Pinking: A metallic noise from the engine often caused by the *ignition timing* being too far advanced. The noise is the result of pressure waves which cause the cylinder walls to vibrate, when the ignited fuel/air is compressed.

Piston: Cylindrical component which slides in a closely-fitting metal tube or *cylinder* and transmits pressure. The pistons in an engine, for example, compress the fuel/air mixture, transmit the combustion power to the *crankshaft,* and exhaust the burnt gases.

Piston ring: Hardened metal ring which is a spring fit in a groove running round the *piston* to ensure a close fit to the *cylinder* wall.

Positive earth: The opposite of *negative earth.*

Propeller shaft: The shaft which transmits the drive from the *gearbox* to the rear axle in front engine/rear wheel drive cars.

Pushrod: A rod which is moved up and down by the rotary motion of the *camshaft* and operates the *rocker arm* in an OHV engine.

Q

Quarter light: A triangular window often mounted in the front door of a car.

Quartz-halogen bulb: A bulb with a quartz envelope (instead of glass) and a tungsten filament, and filled with one of the halogen group of gases (often iodine).

R

Rack and pinion: Simplest form of steering mechanism which uses a *pinion* gear to move a toothed rack.

Radial ply tyre: A tyre in which the tread plies are arranged laterally, at right angles to the circumferential plane.

Radiator: Cooling device, situated in an air flow and comprising a system of fine tubes and fins for rapid heat dissipation, through which engine coolant is passed.

Radius arms (rods): Locating arms sometimes used with a *live axle* to positively locate it in the fore-and-aft direction.

Recirculating ball steering: A derivation of *worm and nut* steering, where the steering shaft motion is transmitted to the steering linkage by balls running in the groove of a worm gear.

Regraded tyres: Previously known as remould qualities (RQ's), these are new tyres with a minor cosmetic fault.

Rev-counter: See *tachometer.*

Rocker arm: A lever which rocks on a central pivot, one end is moved up and down by the *camshaft* action and the other end operates the inlet of exhaust *valve.*

Rotor arm: A rotating arm is the *distributor* which distributes the *HT* spark voltage to the correct *spark plug.*

Running on: A tendency for an engine to keep on running after the ignition has been switched off; it's often caused by a badly maintained engine, or use of an unsuitable grade of fuel.

S

SAE: Society of Automotive Engineers (of America). The SAE classification of oils is well known but, as with *DIN* standards, SAE covers a wide range of measuring output, performance, etc, of motor vehicles.

Safety rim: A special wheel rim shape which prevents a deflated tyre from rolling off the wheel.

Sealed beam: A sealed headlamp unit where the filament is an integral part and cannot be renewed separately. Although much more expensive than separate bulbs, the illumination does not deteriorate due to contamination.

Semi-elliptic spring: A *leaf spring* used for many car rear *suspension* systems.

Semi-trailing arm: A common form of independent rear *suspension* which allows the wheel carrier to be pivoted.

Servo: A device for multiplying the normal effort applied to a control. With a brake servo, this uses the suction created in the engine inlet *manifold* to act on a *diaphragm and pushrod* for additional braking effort; it's attached to the brake *hydraulic master cylinder.*

Shock absorber: A device for damping out the up-and-down movement of a car when the *suspension* hits a bump in the road.

Solid state: A term used in electronics to describe semi-conductor devices (transistors, diodes, integrated circuits, etc). These are used in *alternators, electronic ignition* systems, radios and some instruments.

Semi-idle carburettor: A *carburettor* where the air used for the fuel/air mixture at idle speeds is mixed in a special by-pass tube which increases the pressure drop. The velocity of the mixture increases to above the speed of sound and at the same time it becomes very turbulent which improves the fuel/air atomization.

Spark plug: A device with a ceramic insulator and two electrodes on a common metal body which screws part-way into the engine *combustion chamber.* When the *HT* voltage is applied to the plug terminal, a spark jumps the air-gap at the electrodes.

Squab: Another name for a seat cushion, not the backrest.

Steel-braced tyre: Tyre in which an extra ply containing steel cords is incorporated to give added strength.

Steering arm (knuckle): Short arm on the rear face of the front *stub axle* to which the steering linkage connects.

Steering rack: See *Rack and pinion.*

Stroboscopic light: A light powered from the engine *ignition system* which is used for checking the ignition timing when the engine is running (ie dynamically).

Stoke: The total travel of the *piston* in the bore.

Stub axle. A short axle which carries the wheel only.

Sub-frame: A small frame or chassis which carries the *suspension,* and which in turn is connected to the car body.

Sump: The main oil container at the lowest part of an engine.

Suppressor: a device which is used to suppress or damp-out electrical interference caused by the *ignition system,* or *generator,* wiper motor etc.

Suspension: A general term used to describe the links, springs and *dampers* with which the car body is suspended on the wheels.

Swing axle: A *Suspension* arm which is pivoted near the centre-line of the car, and which gives the wheel a vertical swinging action about that pivot point.

Synchromesh: A device in a *gearbox* which synchronizes the speed of one gear shaft with another to produce smooth, noiseless engagement of the relative gears.

T

Tachometer: Also known as a rev counter, this indicates the engine speed in revolutions per minute (rpm).

Tappet: A term nowadays widely misused to refer to the adjustable part of the valvegear of an engine. True tappets are found only in the valvegear of older engines.

Thermostat: A device which is sensitive to changes in engine temperature, and opens up an additional path for coolant to flow when the engine has warmed up.

Tie-rod (track rod): A general term for a rod which provides location for a component, or between two components (as with steering linkage).

Timing chain: Metal flexible-link chain engaging on sprocket wheels and driving the *camshaft from the crankshaft* in an *OHV* engine.

Timing marks: Marks normally found on the *crankshaft* pulley or *flywheel* and used for setting the ignition fixing point with respect to a particular *piston.*

Toe-in/toe-out: The amount by which the front wheels point inwards or outwards, expressed either as an angle or linear measurement.

Top dead centre (tdc): The point at which a piston is at the top of its stroke.

Torque: The turning effort generated by any rotating part.

Torque converter: A coupling where the driving *torque* is transmitted through oil. At low speeds there is very little transference of torque from the input to the output; as the input shaft speed increases, the direction of fluid flow within a system of vanes alters and torque from the input impeller is transferred to the output turbine. The higher the input speed, the closer the output speed approaches it, until they are virtually the same.

Torsion bar: A spring-steel bar which turns about its own axis, and is used in some independent front *suspension* systems.

Toughened windscreen: A windscreen which will shatter in a particular way to produce blunt-edged fragments or will craze over the remain intact. A zone-toughened windscreen has a zone in front of the driver which crazes into larger parts to reduce the loss of visibility which occurs with toughened windscreens, but is otherwise similar.

Track rod: A rod which connects the steering arms to the steering gear and/or steering idler gear.

Trailing arm: A form of independent *suspension* where the wheel is attached to a swinging arm, and is mounted to the rear of the arm pivot.

Transaxle: A form of combined *gearbox* and axle from which two shafts transmit the drive to the wheels.

Transmission: A general term used for a *gearbox,* but very often used as an alternative for a *transaxle.*

Turning circle: See *leading shoe.*

Two-stroke (cycle): A common term used to describe the operation of an engine where each downward piston stroke is a power stroke. The fuel/air mixture is ported into the crankcase where it's compressed by the descending *piston* and 'pumped' through another port into the *combustion chamber.* As the piston rises, the mixture is compressed and ignited, which forces the piston down. The burnt gases flow from the exhaust port, but the piston is now compressing a further charge in the crankcase which repeats the cycle. The engine needs careful design to prevent the unburnt and burnt gases from mixing and, although not a feature of the simplest designs, in some versions a rotary or reed *valve* is incorporated to help achieve this.

U

Understeer: A tendency for a car to go straight on when turned into a corner.
Universal joint: A joint that can swivel in any direction whilst at the same time transmitting *torque.* It's commonly used in *propeller shafts* and *driveshafts,* but is not suitable for some applications because the input and output shaft speeds are not the same at all positions of angular rotation. The type in common use is known as a *Hardy-Spicer,* Hooke's or Carden joint.
Unsprung weight: That part of a car which is not supported by the springs.
Upper cylinder lubricant (UCL): A type of light oil intended to be added to a car's fuel with the object of providing extra lubrication for the *cylinder* walls.

V

Vacuum advance: System of igntion *advance and retard* used in certain *distributors* where the vacuum in the engine intake *manifold* is transmitted to the distributor and acts on a *diaphragm* to alter the ignition timing according to throttle position.
Vacuum gauge: A device which indicates the amount of vacuum or suctrion in the inlet *manifold.*
Valve: A device which opens or closes to permit or stop gas flow into the engine.
Vee engine: Design in which the *cylinders* of an engine are set in two banks forming a V when viewed from one end. A V8, for example, consists of two such rows of four cylinders each.
Venturi: A streamlined restriction in the *carburettor* throttle bore which causes a low pressure to occur; this sucks fuel into the air stream to form a vapour suitable for combustion.
Viscosity: A term used to describe the resistance of a fluid to flow. When associated with lubricating oil it's given an *SAE* number, 10 being a very light oil and 140 being a very heavy oil.
Viscous coupling: A fluid coupling incorporated in the hub of the cooling fan on some cars. This permits a certain amount of 'slip', so that at higher engine speeds, the fan speed is reduced to lower the noise level and the amount of power taken from the engine.
Voltage regulator: A device which regulates the *generator* output to a predetermined level. For most *alternator* systems this is an integral part of the alternator itself, and therefore mainly applicable to *dynamo* systems. Regulators on later cars also have a device to regulate the charging current as well as the voltage.

W

Wankel engine: A rotary engine originally developed by Felix Wankel which has a triangular shaped rotor in an epitrochoidal housing (approximates in shape to a broad-waisted figure of eight). The engine has never proved popular in production cars in the UK.
Watts linkage: An arrangement of three links sometimes used for the transverse location of *live or de Dion axles.*
Wheel balancing: Adding weights at the rim of a car wheel so that there are no out-of-balance forces.
White metal: A tin or lead based *bearing* material.
Wishbone: An A-shaped *suspension* link, pivoted at the base of the A, and carrying a wheel at the apex. Normally mounted in an approximately horizontal plane.
Worn and nut steering: A steering system where the lower end of the steering column has a coarse screw thread on which a nut runs. The nut is attached to a spindle which carries the drop arm which, in turn, moves the steering linkage.

CONVERSION

Distance

Inches	X	25,400	=	*Millimeters (mm)*
Feet (ft)	X	0.305	=	*Meters (m)*
Miles	X	1.609	=	*Kilometres (km)*
Millimetres (mm)	X	0.039	=	*Inches (in)*
Metres (m)	X	3.281	=	*Feet (ft)*
Kilometres (km)	X	0.621	=	*Miles*

Capacity

Inches, cubic (cu in/in^3)	X	16.387	=	*Centimetres, cubic (cc/cm^3)*
Fluid ounce, imperial (fl oz)	X	35.51	=	*Centimetres, cubic (cc/cm^3)*
Fluid ounce, US (fl oz)	X	29.57	=	*Centimetres, cubic (cc/cm^3)*
Pints, impreial (imp pt)	X	0.568	=	*Litres (L)*
Quarts, imperial (imp qt)	X	1.1365	=	*Litres (L)*
Quarts, imperial (imp qt)	X	1.201	=	*Quart, US (US qt)*
Quarts, US (US qt)	X	0.9463	=	*Litres (L)*
Quarts, US (US qt)	X	0.8326	=	*Quarts, imperial (imp qt)*
Gallons, imperial (imp gal)	X	4.546	=	*Litres (L)*
Gallons, imperial (imp gal)	X	1.201	=	*Gallons, US (US gal)*
Gallons, US (US gal)	X	3.7853	=	*Litres (L)*
Gallons, US (US gal)	X	0.8326	=	*Gallons, imperial (imp gal)*
Centimetres, cubic (cc/cm^3)	X	0.061	=	*Inches cubic in/in^3)*
Centimetres, cubic (cc/cm^3)	X	0.02816	=	*Fluid ounces, imperial (fl oz)*
Centimetres, cubic (cc/cm^3)	X	0.03381	=	*Fluid ounces, US (fl oz)*
Litres (L)	X	28.16	=	*Fluid ounces, imperial (fl oz)*
Litres (L)	X	33.81	=	*Fluid ounces, US (fl oz)*
Litres (L)	X	1.760	=	*Pints, imperial (imp pt)*
Litres (L)	X	0.8799	=	*Quarts, imperial (imp qt)*
Litres (L)	X	1.0567	=	*Quarts, US (US qt)*
Litres (L)	X	0.220	=	*Gallons, imperial (imp gal)*
Litres (L)	X	0.264	=	*Gallons, Us (US gal)*

Area

Inches, square (in^2/sq in)	X	645.160	=	*Millimetres, square (mm^2/sq mm)*
Feet square (ft^2/sq ft)	X	0.093	=	*Metres, square (m^2/sq m)*
Millimetres, square (mm^2/sq mm)	X	0.002	=	*Inches, square (in^2/sq in)*
Metres, square (m^2/sq m)	X	10.764	=	*Feet square (ft^2/sq ft)*

Weight

Ounces (oz)	X	28.350	=	*Grammes (g)*
Pounds (lbs)	X	0.454	=	*Kilogrammes (kg)*
Grammes (g)	X	0.035	=	*Ounces (oz)*
Kilogrammes (kg)	X	2.205	=	*Pounds (lbs)*
Kilogrammes (kg)	X	35.274	=	*Ounces (oz)*

FACTORS

Pressure

Pounds/sq in (psi/lb/sq in/ lb/in^2)	X	0.070	=	*Kilogrammes/sq cm (kg/sq cm)*
Pounds/sq in (psi/lb/sq in/ lb/in^2)	X	0.068	=	*Atmospheres (atm)*
Kilogrammes sq cm (kg/sq cm)	X	14.223	=	*Pounds/sq in (psi/lb/sq in/ lb/in^2)*
Atmospheres (atm)	X	14.696	=	*Pounds/sq in (psi/lb/sq in lb/in^2)*

Torque

Pound – inches (lbf in)	X	0.0115	=	*Kilogramme – metres (kgf m)*
Pound – inches (lbf in)	X	0.0833	=	*Pound – feet (lbf ft)*
Pound – feet (lbf ft)	X	12	=	*Pound – inches (lbf in)*
Pound – fet (lbf ft)	X	0.138	=	*Kilogramme – metres (kgf m)*
Pound – feet (lbf ft)	X	1.356	=	*Newton – metres (Nm)*
Kilogramme – metres (kgf m)	X	86.796	=	*Pound – inches (lbf in)*
Kilogramme – metres (kgf m)	X	7.233	=	*Pound – feet (lbf ft)*
Newton – metres (Nm)	X	0.738	=	*Pound – feet (lbf ft)*
Newton – metres (Nm)	X	0.102	=	*Kilogramme – metres (kgf m)*

Speed

Miles – hour (mph)	X	1.609	=	*Kilometres – hour (kph)*
Feet – second	X	0.305	=	*Metres – second (m/s)*
Kilometres – hour (kph)	X	0.621	=	*Miles – hour (mph)*
Metres – second (m/s)	X	3.281	=	*Feet – second*
Metres – second (m/s)	X	3.600	=	*Kilometres – hour (kph)*

Consumption

Miles - gallon, imperial (mpg)	X	0.354	=	*Kilometres – litre (km/l)*
Kilometres – litre (km/l)	X	2.825	=	*Miles – gallon, imperial (mpg)*

Temperature

Centigrade (°C) to Farenheit (°F)	$\frac{9}{5}(°C + 32) = °F$
Farenheit (°F) to Centigrade (°C)	$\frac{5}{9}(°F - 32) = °C)$

Index

Printed by
Haynes Publishing Group
Sparkford Yeovil Somerset
England